WILD ANIMALS AROUND YOUR HOME

WILD ANIMALS AROUND YOUR HOME

Paul Villiard

Winchester Press

Library of Congress Catalog Card Number: 74-16877
ISBN: 0-87691-170-X

Published by Winchester Press
460 Park Avenue, New York 10022

Printed in the United States of America

For Annette Villiard

Contents

Preface   8

1
Wild Animals as Pets   11

2
Wild Animals as Pests   23

3
Attracting Animals
to Your Property   33

4
Animal Diets and Habits   47

5
Reptiles and Amphibians   74

6
Some Animal Stories   100

Appendix:
Animals and the Law   141

Index   157

Preface

It is surprising to find out how very little the average suburban or rural homeowner knows about the natural history and behavior of most of the small animals which have adjusted to life near or about his own house.

With the increasing trend toward suburban living, more and more of these creatures are being observed—mostly for the first time—by people who have no knowledge at all about them. Even in this age of enlightenment it is the exceptional person who has any firsthand information about the creatures with whom he shares the earth. And not only is this the case, but people who are not completely uninformed are nevertheless often misinformed—full of superstitions and old wives' tales, some of them little short of astonishing.

It seems to be time for mankind to take a hard look at his environment, and at the creatures coinhabiting it. Up to very recently man's attitude has been not that these creatures are sharing the world with him, but that they are occupying space and using food that was put there for his sole and exclusive benefit. This is at the very best a shortsighted outlook for which the holders are not necessarily to blame, having had these beliefs handed down to them through the years and generations.

It is simply amazing to discover how tenacious are some of the stories dealing with living things around us. It is impossible to trace the origin of most of them, and the patent lack of credibility in these stories is apparent only to others—never to the persons telling them.

The purpose of this book is to inform the reader audience about the behavior of these little creatures, to tell some of the facts about them and their lives—I must repeat, facts, not fancies—and, above all, to attempt to scotch a few of the truly weird tales still spread about them. If only a few persons are afforded a new outlook toward their furred, feathered, and scaled cousins after reading the chapters within these covers, then I will feel I have achieved a real measure of success in the writing of this book, and have made a valuable contribution toward the better understanding and tolerance of our ecological partners.

—Paul Villiard
Saugerties, New York
1974

Chapter
1

Wild Animals
as Pets

One of the situations that can confront the new sub-
urbanite occurs so frequently that it is almost uni-
versal. Mr. Jones moves to the country, and, even
before the family is settled in their new home, Johnny
comes breathlessly into the house hugging an animal
to his chest. "Can I keep it for a pet, Daddy?"

The animal may be anything—a baby raccoon, a
snake, a patient skunk who has not been frightened
enough to let Johnny know what a skunk can do to the
unwary. It will probably be a young immature creature, since picking up an adult wild animal is nearly

11

impossible. Being a juvenile, it will be cute and cuddly. Almost all baby animals are cute and cuddly. However, many cute and cuddly baby animals have the disconcerting habit of growing up into great *big* animals, often fierce and unmanageable.

This last factor is not the one that immediately interests the Joneses, however. The problem at hand is what to do with the animal. What to do for it. How to handle it. How to see that it is given the proper conditions needed for survival and comfort.

Naturally, the very best thing that could be done for the creature is to have little Johnny take it back to the *exact* place he found it, give it a nice pat, and release it. Ninety-nine out of a hundred "lost" animals are not lost. They are being trained either to hunt for food or in another point of survival by the adult animals at the time Johnny stumbles across them. At the approach of the child, the adults quietly fade away. With man's dull senses, Johnny has no idea that there are other animals in the vicinity except the one he has "found," wandering about in a more or less bewildered fashion.

Now, one of two things is going to happen. Either the boy will be allowed to keep the animal, or the boy's mother is going to see a wild animal in the grasp of her son and immediately jump into a fit of the screaming meemies, and she may even try to snatch the animal away from Johnny to commit mayhem upon its innocent being.

Either way, my sympathy goes out to Johnny, because he has the great misfortune to have been born into a family which will train him just as surely as there are little apples either to damage his environment by well-intentioned ignorance or to fear crea-

This cute little bundle will make a nice pet until he grows up. Then he will probably become irritable and hard to manage. Better to let him roam free.

tures and to destroy them on sight, as if from a self-protective instinct. (But such destruction certainly is not instinct—it is a conditioned reaction, an induced fear that the mother has passed to her son and that can be passed on and on and on through the family line, unless some generation is brought up short somewhere along the way by facts.)

All too often, parents make the first mistake and are too permissive to their offspring. Johnny is permitted to keep the animal he brought home. Usually this marks the beginning of a period of pure misery for the poor creature. First is the matter of proper food. What do you feed a strange creature—one that perhaps no one in the entire family has ever seen outside a zoo or game farm? If the young animal happens to be a skunk, the feeding problem is not apt to come up, of course. At the first screech and the first wild motion toward the cute and cuddly little thing, the skunk will let go with his defense mechanism, and he has a good one! Mommy and Johnny and anyone else in the room at the time will not be thinking of food for a day or so, and it may be as long as a week before they will be able to move back into the house.

But if the animal is unfortunate enough to have fallen into the hands of a child of doting parents, what *will* they feed it? The diet of wild animals is a lot different from that of a domesticated animal like a cat or a dog. Yet many of these unwilling "pet" animals are fed on such a diet. True, they will survive, sometimes for a long time, on a diet unsuitable for them, which merely speaks well for their strength of will to live. And the things I have had people tell me that wild animals eat are fantastic. As an example, one man, otherwise rather sensible, told me that the only food raccoons ate was garbage. Upon being asked how

Sometimes a baby squirrel will fall out of its nest and be abandoned by its parents—in which case it is no cruelty to try to raise it, though it is a lot of work.

he came to that conclusion his reply was that all the raccoons around his place ate nothing but the garbage out of his cans! Not a single 'coon had been seen eating fresh food of any kind. Well, that was a brilliant deduction on his part, but then I asked him if he ever put out any fresh food for the little visitors. He looked at me as though I were some kind of a nut.

Certainly raccoons, and nearly any other animal, too, will raid your garbage can when they are hungry enough, or when they have been unable to find food for themselves. Usually the reason they were unable to bring down any prey was that you had built your house, and your neighbors had done the same, right smack in the middle of their hunting preserve, driving away all the game on which wild animals would normally have survived.

It is very difficult for an animal to pull up stakes and move to another territory when you pull up your own stakes and move into his. As uncivilized as mankind still is, we have at least reached the point where we *can* move into a strange territory without having to kill the people already living there, or at the very least beat them up and drive them away to make room for ourselves. Animals have not reached that point. Each animal has a given range. The size of the range is determined by the amount of food needed for survival by any given animal, and by the amount of that food on the range. In locations where game is scarce, the range is necessarily a lot larger than it is in localities where game is plentiful.

Now, within his own range, each animal moves about freely and comfortably, at peace with his neighbors and with other animals occupying the same range—*as long as they are not of his same species.* Since each kind of animal—with, of course, some exceptions—eats a different kind of food, one species does not infringe upon the foraging or hunting opportunities of another species, even though both animals live in the same territory.

Take the case of a raccoon. The range of this animal is about 200 acres. This means that a territory this size will support one raccoon comfortably, but will not support two. As long as that animal remains in his territory he will be all right. But if he wanders into the territory bordering his own, the chances are he will be attacked by the raccoon living in the adjoining land. This is nothing less than simple survival. The other raccoon would have been attacked by the first one if he had wandered over the border.

And even when attack takes place, there is seldom any damage done to either animal. Almost without exception, the individual who is trespassing on the other's territory gives way after the first warning and prudently retreats onto his own land. As soon as he is across the border the attack ceases and both animals go on about their own business as though the incident had not occurred. No grudge is held; as a matter of fact, it is very doubtful if either specimen remembers what happened after an hour or two.

That is the way wild animals feed in their natural surroundings. Obviously, even if you can provide the proper diet, a wild "pet" is not going to feel much like eating out of a dog dish while the big noisy creatures who have just captured it crowd around.

So the animal's future does not appear too bright, right from the start. What about Johnny's welfare?

Many people are concerned about diseases which may be transmitted to human beings by one kind of wild animal or another. For the most part, diseases common to animals are not transmissable to human beings. There are a few exceptions, such as psittacosis or "parrot fever." The incidence of parrot fever is so small, however, that you can forget about it almost completely. Some animals contract rabies, and a person bitten by a rabid animal may also contract the disease. Again, however, the chance of being bitten by a rabid wild animal is remote, and need not be a source of fear in rural areas. One is much more likely to be bitten by a rabid dog or cat than by any other animal. Skunks, foxes, squirrels, raccoons, and some species of bats are some of the wild animals which have been known to be rabid at times. The danger is very slight, though. First of all, it is difficult in the extreme to get close enough to a wild animal to be bitten, since the first thought that any animal has on sighting a human being is to flee as though he were pursued by the very devil, which, to the animal, he is.

Tularemia is a disease transmitted to man by rabbits, and it can be fatal. It is contracted by handling rabbits infected by the disease. For this reason it is a good idea not to handle wild rabbits, or eat them. Far safer to stick to domestic breeds, which seem to be free of the ailment.

Other diseases which can be transmitted from animals to human beings are very few, and they present no danger if one uses just a minimal amount of common sense. If a wild animal is obviously sick it will show it, and you just leave it alone. If a domesticated animal is sick it shows it too, and one usually calls in a veterinarian. Only rarely do we do the same for a wild creature.

Parasites are not really the same as disease in wild animals, and as a matter of fact, there are very few wild animals which do not have a flourishing colony of fleas, mites, ticks, or other bloodsucking pests infesting their fur or feathers. Even reptiles have mites and ticks which lodge under the scales of the animal, causing it no end of misery. These pestiferous hitchhikers do not as a rule live on human beings. It is possible that they can carry diseases that would infect man if the bacterium or virus got into the bloodstream, but again, there is a very slight possibility of this happening, because in order for it to occur, we would have to be in very close contact with the animal long enough for the flea or other critter to transfer to our own body, then have the thing bite us. Again, minimal common sense would eliminate most of this possibility.

One hazard that must be taken into consideration is completely the fault of people, not animals. Some people, in an apparent ecstasy of affection for all living creatures, will seize a wild animal, hug it to their breast, or even worse, kiss it. Such ebullience is entirely out of place when handling animals of any species except the young of the human race. This is one excellent way to catch a sickness if the animal happens to be infected with something that can be transmitted to human beings.

You should know what to expect when you encounter an animal around your home in a suburban area— or in an urban area too, for that matter, since often a stray creature will become hopelessly tangled up in a housing development and wander into your yard. Each animal will react characteristically upon sighting its hereditary enemy.

Usually, if the creature is a juvenile, nothing will happen. Most of the time it will just amble away, but slowly enough to permit you to overtake it. This is not to imply that it *wants* you to overtake it. I merely mean that it has not yet learned to fear you, so it is in no hurry to escape. If, indeed, you do overtake it and pick it up, the chances are that it will not try to do anything to defend itself, other than to become a squirming handful of animation, since practically no wild creature likes to be picked up.

Before we enlarge upon the possible behavior when approached, let me explain what an animal feels upon capture. While, as I said just above, a juvenile animal has not yet learned fear of human beings, it does have one very real instinctive fear, and this is the fear of confinement. Perhaps here, the word "instinctive" is misused, because it takes countless years—thousands or tens of thousands perhaps—for any reaction to become an instinct in any species of animal. The fear of confinement may have been developed only since mankind began to trap other animals, in which case it would be an acquired fear rather than an instinct.

However the animal learned this fear, the point is that it has it, to a considerable degree. Confinement to an animal means a trap. A trap means death. It is as simple as that. Consequently, an animal which may stand patiently to let you pet it as much as you desire may very well, upon being picked up, turn and try to bite, since biting and clawing are its natural defenses. This action would naturally be more quick and more severe in the case of an adult animal.

All this is not to say that a wild animal cannot be picked up. There are ways to pick up such creatures without throwing them into a frenzy of fear and attempts to escape. The action of your hands is most important when handling an animal. If you approach an animal with your hands outstretched over it, this is an attack. Many of an animal's enemies attack it from above. If you approach with rapid motions, this is also an attack, since an animal trying to catch its prey must necessarily make rapid motions—more rapid than the prey, or it would not fare very well.

If you grasp the creature, wrapping your hands around its body, this is entrapment and confinement, spelling *danger* in loud tones to the creature. Also, if you happen to be a smoker and smoke while you are investigating a wild animal, you may start something you cannot well handle, since smoke puffed into the face of an animal means fire. Fire is one of the worst dangers in the life of a wild creature, and an ill-advised puff of cigarette smoke into the vision of an animal may very well drive it into a veritable frenzy of fear, together with an appropriate cyclonic attempt to escape. If at the time you happen to have your hands around it or near it, you are very liable to sustain some good lacerations.

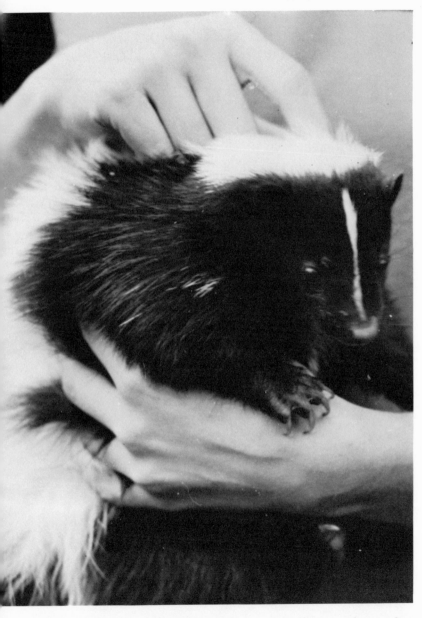

Even skunks can be handled without fear if you do not make any fast motions or loud noises. Offer a tidbit—they love apple—and you may make a friend.

All of the admonitions in this chapter have not been intended to cause you to lock yourself in the attic whenever you see a little creature nibbling in your garbage can. What they are intended to do is make you aware that there are correct ways to approach animals, and that there is not as much to fear from them as you might think or might have been taught in your childhood.

After you have learned something about such creatures, you can begin to enjoy their presence. The more you learn about them, the more fascinating they become, and, after you have had some experience with one or two species, you will more than probably become so interested in their behavior and daily lives that you will search out other kinds to observe and will try to attract them to the vicinity of your home. In a sense they will be pets—but not caged or domesticated pets.

Chapter 2

Wild Animals as Pests

In the first chapter we have been discussing creatures from the point of view of their being desired visitors and possible pets around your rural home. There is, however, another aspect—the nuisance these otherwise charming creatures can be.

Anyone who has had his attic invaded by red squirrels will immediately know what I am talking about. The amount of destruction a colony of these endearing little beasties can wreak in a short time is absolutely astonishing.

Of course, if you build your own home—or at least, have it built and oversee most of the construction—you can pay particular attention to the sealing up of all points of entrance that may otherwise be left open. Spaces under the overhang soffits are the favorite places of entry for squirrels. The red squirrel has the worst reputation for house invasion, although the gray squirrel and the chipmunk also perform depredations in attics, garages, and basements.

The mating season is the time when most of these animals come inside a home. They are merely looking for safe places in which to build nests to rear their young. Finding a whole world of wonderful materials such as stored linens, clothing, bedding, camping gear, and whatever, it is no wonder that the simple little animals go out of their tree, so to speak. They chew up everything they can sink their teeth into. If the things are packed in boxes, no matter; they first chew their way into the container, then proceed to annihilate the contents. Mice and rats do the same, but they are less often found in high places like an attic. Their usual point of entry is the cellar or basement, or on the ground floor of the house proper.

As much as a squirrel may delight you by doing acrobatics outside in the old pine tree, or amusingly chewing open a walnut in its paws while the entire family watches with pleasure, that same squirrel is enough to drive you to your gun cabinet with rage in your heart when you discover it has made its nest smack in the middle of your box of best winter clothes, chewing them up until they are shredded into soft downy stuff for the darling little babies to cuddle in. I might add that a squirrel's nest, also, is not the cleanest of places, so what clothes were not chewed to fragments may very well be soiled beyond redemption.

24

And the destruction does not stop there! If one of the creatures decides that other pastures in the attic are greener than the one he has entered, he thinks nothing at all of climbing down inside the walls hunting for new horizons to explore. Finding his way blocked by the studding, he can, and often does, chew right through two-by-fours, causing a weakening in the wall at that point which may or may not give way at any future date when a strain builds up in the building because of settlement or other natural causes.

The red squirrel is an appealing fellow—*outdoors*. They can quickly destroy the contents of an attic and even damage the structure of a house. (Photo: Ontario Dept. of Lands & Forests)

It is disconcerting to see an area in the wall suddenly crack open, and to find on investigation that a couple of studs have been chewed in half. The damage is often extensive, and large portions of the framing have to be torn out in order to replace the damaged members.

We live in a huge rambling house of my own construction. I have been building it for twelve years, and at last have only one more addition to build in order to complete the structure. During all this time it has been impossible for me to block all holes where small animals can find entrance. As a consequence, we have been unwilling hosts to a truly remarkable assortment of creatures. The house is built in the middle of woods that I had to clear of trees in order to build, and these same woods abound in wildlife, even though we are only a few miles from a village. Also, living in such close proximity to wildlife ranges has given me a wonderful opportunity for observation.

When I say "unwilling hosts," perhaps I am not being exactly honest about my feelings, since I personally do not begrudge the animals shelter and/or food. My wife takes a somewhat dimmer view of these invasions, and rightly so, since the cleanup falls on her for the most part, and the damaged items are sometimes things she feels rather strongly about losing. However, even she is somewhat lenient in her reaction and condemnation of the little furry friends, after her first flash of rage has passed.

We have everything from white-footed mice giving birth to their litters in the pantry, to corn snakes happily roaming around our living-room floor. Baby corn snakes, at that! A flying squirrel presented us with five down-soft babies in the boiler room. We often find the intact skins of snakes high on the plates of partition walls, left there when their owners came in out of the elements to find a safe place to crawl out of them.

Admittedly these sorts of experiences could cause a city dweller some concern if not actual distress. When I first married, my wife was a true city girl. She was born in New York City, and had been out of it only once or twice, and then only for short trips to other cities. She had actually never seen a living cow! I was born in Washington State and spent my youth also in cities, but in cities where I had access to woodsy areas and great parks. I was an eager investigator of everything that moved, wiggled, flew, or swam, and I have come to know much about the creatures living on this planet with me. I might add that my longsuffering wife has made admirable strides to keep up with my ecological activities, and has come to accept most of the creatures with aplomb if not actual enjoyment.

The fall is the time when most of these animals try to invade the house. Nights are getting cold, food is becoming scarce, and a small opening into an invitingly warm place is not ignored. Among the first strangers are the white-footed mice. These common field mice differ from the common house mouse in that the underparts are pure white, and they are a bit larger. They are not as wild and wary as the house mouse. They are also called deer mice.

They build elaborate nests out of almost any material, including your stored summer clothes if they happen to get into the location where you keep them. Even so, their destruction is far less than the house mouse or the vole, sometimes called the meadow mouse. Unless they happen to step into the traps, we do not kill white-footed mice when we encounter them in the house, but catch them and liberate them outdoors. One reason is that they consume a great quantity of insects as part of their normal diet, and, if you ever live in a rural area, anything that eats insects pays its own way, as far as I am concerned.

Voles, or meadow mice, look very much like mice at a quick glance, but they are easily distinguished by their abbreviated tail, a tiny, stubby little thing compared with the tail of a regular mouse. Voles are much more destructive than the common mouse, and they eat their own weight in plant material per day. Very little if any insect food is consumed, so these creatures have not the saving trait of being of service for their keep. They breed at a prodigious rate, each female producing 100 or more babies each year!

The vole destroys more than three million tons of hay each year, making it the scourge of farmers depending on hay crops for their stock and for sale. They destroy trees, especially fruit trees, by girdling them. Girdling a tree consists of eating the bark from the trunk in a band completely encircling the trunk. This effectively cuts off the flow of sap and sugars up and down the trunk, isolating the leaves from their nourishment. The tree is therefore dead after girdling, and the next year will remain a leafless bare structure. Hard winters see many trees girdled by voles under the snow, the girdling not becoming apparent until the snow has melted to reveal the trunk down to the ground.

The vole tunnels run every which way deep under the surface, leading from tree to tree. In such winters deer also will girdle trees to keep from starving, although this is not the usual practice of deer.

Another animal which sometimes causes grief in the suburban habitat is the mole. Ordinarily you would never see this secretive and subterranean animal. As a matter of fact, you don't even see it when it does its damage, which is to run tunnels all under your lawns. The trouble is, the tunnels are so near the surface that they cause long, winding ridges to appear everywhere the creature burrows. Grass roots can be damaged by the digging process, to say nothing of

Chipmunks can be a pest both in your house and in your garden. But if you have a tight attic and protect your flower bulbs with screening, you can happily coexist with them.

your breaking an ankle when you step on a tunnel and the dirt caves in under your weight.

I don't know of any way to discourage moles from tunneling your lawn, except to throw conservation to the winds and set a mole trap at the most likely place to impale the poor creature as it ambles along looking for a succulent earthworm for breakfast. The only trouble with killing off the moles, however, is that they are valuable allies because insects compose the major part of their diet, and injurious grubs a large part of that percentage. You must make the choice between a ridge across your lawn, or the removal of a great many critters which would otherwise invade your shrubbery and gardens.

Chipmunks are delightful little animals, performing like miniature squirrels in festive raiment. Until they invade your attic and chew up everything. Moreover, if you are a flower lover and wish to set out a number of bulbs each year, forget it if you also have chipmunks around. Chipmunks spend a great deal of time chatteringly thanking you for your bulb planting, and they proceed to dig up and devour them as fast as you put them into the ground. They won't miss a single one.

Through experience we have learned that the only way to ensure your bulb flowers' survival amid a colony of chipmunks is to plant them under an impenetrable screen. My wife and I use ½-inch-mesh hardware cloth, and the system is very simple. You cultivate the location where you wish the bulbs to grow, then remove as much topsoil as the depth of planting indicates. In other words, if the bulbs should be planted 6 inches deep, this much soil should be scooped out. Now stand the bulbs up in the place you want them, and lay a piece of hardware cloth over them, first sifting the soil back until it is just level with the tops of the bulbs. The hardware-cloth screen should extend not less than a foot in every direction farther than the bulb planting. Now replace the soil on top of the screen and stand back to watch the fun. It will not take long for the busy and inquisitive little creatures to sniff out your bulbs. Then they rapidly dig down to get them. Their language is shocking when they come to the screen. Baffled by the barrier, they sit in the dirt and call you every name in the chipmunk vocabulary—but your bulbs will sprout and make their flowers.

Of course, as soon as the flowers are well above ground, you have rabbits to contend with. But be of good cheer. There are sprays that will keep rabbits away from your flowers and shrubbery. Away from your garden, too, if you think the cost of the spray is worth it. Fencing the garden is a better and cheaper way to keep rabbits away from your beans.

Often a bird will take it into her rattlebrained head to build a nest in what seems to you to be the most inconvenient spot on your entire property. One could easily imagine that the bird spent the greater part of her time hunting for the location that would cause you the most inconvenience. Phoebes are noted for this, and a little later on in this volume I will relate my feud with one of these little creatures. The reason why phoebes are such nuisances is that they like to build around human habitats—barns, garages, wellhouses, springhouses, and the like.

The construction of the nest is not so bad. What is bad is that baby phoebes, in common with nearly every other species of baby bird, lift their little rear ends over the edge of the nest and let go, performing this duty, it seems, every few minutes—usually just as you walk under the nest, or at least it seems that way. Woe to the finish of your car if a pesky bird decides to make her nest on the light fixture inside your garage.

The only way you can discourage the practice is to tear out the nest as soon as you see it being built. The bird will immediately commence to build another nest, sometimes in a different place. If the second place is also annoying to you, rip it out again. Once more the persistent critter will make a new one, and, finally, she will choose a place that will permit you to share your property with her without a bombardment from above.

Once in a great while someone will move to a loca-

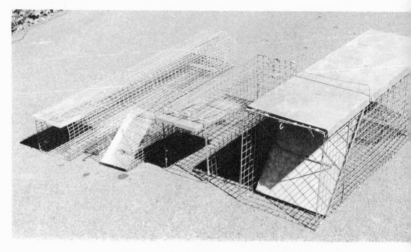

An assortment of nonlethal traps that can be used to catch animals that become a nuisance on your property.

tion that is literally overrun with rats. Perhaps it is close by the town landfill area, or to a supermarket or to some other rodent attraction. This condition is especially bothersome to those who open a small country store. There seems to be no real way of exterminating the animals. Poison placed around will kill a great number, true, but they usually die in the walls and crevices, where they create such a stink as to drive everybody away until the carcasses are dried up. A way has been developed to alleviate this condition, with a supersonic device called Rat-I-Cator, which operates much the same way as a dog whistle. You cannot hear it, but the rats and mice can, and they cannot tolerate the sound, so they leave for the tall timber of their own accord. If you would like more information on the device, a stamped addressed envelope sent to Colvin Systems, P.O. Box 363, Lancaster, Pennsylvania 17604 will bring you written information and prices.

Chapter
3

Attracting Animals to Your Property

It is only fair to warn of the nuisance some animals can be, but I hope that the preceding chapter has not discouraged your interest in having wild animals around your home. In this chapter—and indeed for the rest of the book—we will return to a positive view.

While many wild creatures in suburban areas will at times come to the vicinity of homes to look for food in the refuse cans, many more can be attracted by putting food that they like in places where they can easily find it. The important thing to remember is that you are making an attempt to entice a wild creature out into the comparative open of the yard around a house, and this may not be done in one swoop. You must work up to it.

The best way to go about it is to place tidbits of food at the border of your yard where the field, woods, or other shelter for animals begins. You will find that soon the food will have disappeared during the night. This placement must be repeated each night for several nights in a row.

Then place the food just a little closer to your house. Every three or four nights put the food closer, until finally you are putting out the banquet close enough to enable you to observe the animal taking it.

Before I go any further with this discussion, I might caution you that if you have a dog, forget the wild creatures. The smell alone of a dog is enough to keep them all far away from your place. The hullabaloo a dog usually raises when it smells an animal approaching will finish the trick.

After many nights of food offerings the animal will learn to come regularly for its handout. If you place the food out at the same time each day, you will find that the animal will come at nearly the same time to get it.

It is important that the food for each species of animal be food which is part of its regular and proper diet. It would certainly not attract an animal very well if you put out things completely foreign to its diet. Still, you will find that a wild creature will eat nearly anything digestible when it is hungry, and wild animals are very often hungry, especially around houses, since much if not all of the natural prey has been driven away by the building of those houses. In the next chapter I will advise you on the various diets of many of the animals you are likely to see in suburban areas.

After the creature has become accustomed to finding the food each day, or each night, as the case may be, you may begin your approachment program. You now do not put out the food until the animal has arrived in search of it. As soon as you see it around, put the food out, making no fast motions, and above all, not looking directly at the animal. Just slowly and casually walk out and put down the food, letting the creature see you do it.

This must continue until the animal remains while you position the food. At first, as soon as you appear the little fellow will scamper out of sight to safety. Out of your sight, that is. Rest assured you are still in the creature's line of vision.

After a bit, the creature you are attempting to observe will remain in sight while you place its food. After several days it may even approach a little closer, waiting for you to leave the food so it can come and get it. When this time arrives you have crossed the main hurdle toward making a friend out of the wild creature.

It is now only a matter of time and patience on your part until you will be able to place the dish of food right down under the nose of your furred friend of the wild! The satisfaction of doing so for the first time is a most rewarding experience to anyone at all interested in animal behavior.

Talking to an animal does a lot to alleviate its fear. You can say anything you like, since the creature will not understand a single word. Reciting the multiplication tables is just as good as speaking sentences. The important thing to remember is to talk in a soft voice, but pitched a little higher than usual, since the hearing range of almost all animals you are liable to encounter is higher than that of a human being.

It is very probably the soothing tones of a person speaking to them that quiets their fear. At any rate, it has been shown many times over that a steady, soft monologue when working with a wild creature helps immeasurably to keep it calm and relatively unafraid.

One thing that the novice naturalist often overlooks, or does not even know about, is the pattern of behavior in animals. All animals have a set pattern. These patterns have been set over millennia through survival success or failure. Finally they become instinctive, and the animal will always react the same way to the same stimuli. Not every animal will react the same way. By this I mean not every *species* will react the same way to the same stimulus. What will frighten a raccoon, for example, will merely cause a skunk to look up inquisitively, then shuffle along as though no interference were present.

Either by studying the creature's life history or by direct observation, you will, after becoming familiar with the behavior patterns of any kind of animal, be able to tell when a specimen deviates from that pattern.

Such deviation is not normal. Deviation of any kind indicates that something is not as it should be. In the case of a wild animal, if the creature is adult, abnormal actions often indicate sickness. Such animals should be left strictly alone. Sometimes an animal will react strangely through injury rather than an illness. Many, many animals are struck each day by cars along our roads. Not all of them are killed. Some are injured enough to prevent them from hunting for game, but not enough to cause their death. I feel very sorry for these, because they are doomed to a lingering death from starvation when they are unable to catch their food. The kindest thing that can happen to them is to be found by one of their own predators, which will quickly kill the suffering creature for its own food.

Lures are another way of attracting animals. These are scents which are relished by particular creatures. Musk, fish oils, and many other animal derivatives are used to cure traps by fur hunters. Unfortunately, these lures, while they may attract the animals to them, fail to hold them after they arrive. They might be useful to bring an animal within range to obtain photographs but the specimen will rapidly take off as soon as the shutter clicks.

Sometimes a wild animal may be attracted to a human location by a similar animal held in captivity. If the captive animal is a pet and tame enough to handle and play with, often a wild creature will come to visit, and, if it is compatible with the captive, help itself to some of the food placed for the pet.

Such was the case with a squirrel I had at one time. The story of that animal will be told later on in this book, but I can state here that when Pogo was finally set free to run outside, she brought a steady stream of boy and girl friends back home with her each day, and these soon became tame enough to permit my petting them or otherwise touching them as they sat on the windowsill.

If you feed animals to entice them to your land, there is one thing you must never forget. Animals learn to depend on food put out regularly for them. Those animals and birds which normally would leave your locality seasonally for warmer climates will often remain as long as food is plentiful. In the case of birds, especially, many of the migrating species will fail to migrate if you feed them with any degree of regularity.

There is nothing wrong in this, provided you *continue* to feed them through the winter. Failure to do so will result in the death of the creatures. Many people do not realize this. At their summer homes they feed the birds daily, right up until the fall or the winter, when they close up their houses and return to their city dwellings. As they do so they are signing death warrants for all the migratory birds they have been feeding during the warm months. Those birds will have their migratory instinct broken.

This is a good place to tell you something about instincts in animals. We misuse the word "instinct" constantly in our regular speech. We use the word when we really mean to say "reaction." "Instinct" is the result of evolutionary development in any species of animal. Each instinctive action is triggered by what went before it.

If the chain of action is broken because of outside interference, the creature is usually unable to pick up where it left off, and to continue its normal course of action. It must go back to the very beginning and start all over again.

As an illustration, take a bird during the nesting season. She mates, then builds her nest. Often these two actions are reversed; some birds will build their nests and then mate. However it is worked, there is a definite schedule maintained. The mating action triggers the nest-building instinct. The completion of the nest triggers the egg-laying instinct. Remove the eggs and replace them with anything round and smooth, from marbles to jellybeans, and the bird will continue to set those foreign objects just as faithfully as she did her own eggs.

When the chicks hatch, a new set of instincts becomes apparent—in the chicks, that is. As the mother bird forages for food, the chicks lie quietly huddled in the bottom of the nest. The slight movement of the nest caused by the mother alighting on it with food triggers the feeding instinct in the chicks, and up pop their scrawny necks, their mouths gaping open at the end of them. Usually they begin to peep as loudly as they can. This is to attract the attention of the mother bird to themselves. Usually the loudest and most insistent chick is the first one fed. Often only this one chick is fed until its crop is stuffed to repletion. Only then do the next loudest get their share, and so on down the line to the littlest or weakest, which is fed last of all.

If a chick falls out of the nest it is usually doomed— not necessarily by predators, although this is the cause of many deaths of chicks, but because the instinct chain was broken. The chick lying on the ground, or even on the branch holding the nest, does not feel the triggering shake as the mother bird alights with food. As a consequence, it does not stretch up and gape for food.

On the other hand, the mother, even though she can see the chick lying right out in plain view, ignores it because it is not demanding food, and it cannot occur to the mother bird to go and offer food to a quiescent baby. Consequently, the bird starves to death, or dies of cold, or is snapped up by a predator.

A very interesting fact that relates to the feeding instinct has recently been discovered. It seems that red is a triggering color in birds. At the sight of the red gaping mouths before it, the mother bird rams food down the gullet. A feeding mother bird will also ram food at a red-painted spot placed in the nest at the approximate level of a chick's mouth. To induce captive nectar-feeding birds to go to their feeders, a circle of metal, cardboard, or wood is placed at the end of the feeder with a hole cut out to admit the mouth of the feeder to be reached. On the circle is painted a red flower. This can be the crudest kind of painting, just a few patches of red, resembling petals surrounding the opening to the feeder. The honey-creepers, hummingbirds, sunbirds, or whatever species is being maintained will readily go to the "flower" to sip the nectar from the center. Nectar-feeding butterflies will perform the same actions, feeding from tubes set in the middle of a few painted petals, while completely ignoring identical tubes without the flowers painted around them.

The main point of this discussion is to emphasize the fact that animals act by a given set of rules. In the case, once more, of migratory birds being fed through the summer, the combination of weather and gradual lessening of food supply triggers their migration instinct. Since cold, per se, does not bother birds too much, it follows that the main trigger must be lack of food. If, then, you supply food in practically unlimited amounts—at least regularly every day or so—it follows that the cue needed to send the birds on their way will not occur and the bird will automatically remain in the vicinity where it is being fed.

Then you go home to the city.

Boom goes the axe! The bird would have to go back to the beginning, feeding through the summer, experiencing a gradual lessening of food supply and the onset of cold weather, in order to depart on its migration.

All of this boils down to one simple caution. Do not begin to feed any wild creature unless you are able and willing to continue that feeding right through the winter months. Or, if you simply cannot exist without the presence of attracted wild creatures around your home, and you are there only during the summer months, then stop the feeding not later than early August, so that the animals and birds can go through the all-important triggering sequences.

Depending, of course, on the size of the land you have and on its topography, you can do much toward

Rabbits find wintertime sustenance along the uncleared edges of fields. Note the fox tracks entering from right. (Photo: Leonard Lee Rue III)

making it attractive to wildlife. If you have a pond on it, so much the better, because by judicious planting around the borders of the water you can create a mini-marsh, or an ecosystem for waterfowl, which, you will find, will very shortly discover it and put it to good use.

A few ripe cattail heads shredded along the edge of the water in one strip will soon yield a dense thicket of tall reeds to delight such creatures as red-winged blackbirds and other reed-loving birds. Each planting area need not be large, but should be as large as you can make it commensurate with the total area of your holdings. Much can be done on an acre or two, and much more, naturally, if you have many acres of land. A few blueberry bushes planted where they can keep their "feet" wet will thrive and in a year or two afford food for a great variety of creatures, birds as well as bears.

A couple of apple trees planted well away from the house, down near water if possible, will be sure to bring hungry deer to your place. Deer are inordinately fond of apples. Seed grasses and grains can be scattered in long rows or rectangular plots, making sure that these are near cover of trees or woods rather than right out in the open. Such plantings are annual crops, and must be renewed each year. They afford nourishment for birds of all kinds, game birds as well as songbirds and waterfowl. Small animals also like grains; corn especially will bring raccoons, 'possums, skunks, and other small mammals. If you put out a dozen tomato plants you will delight the hearts of a colony of woodchucks.

These plantings should be made with the idea in mind that they are designed for the wildlife you wish to have around your place, and not for human consumption. That way you will be entirely free of resentment when the animals make good use of the fruits of your labors. Your own gardens should be protected from the invasion of wild things.

If you are not just living in a rural area but are actually farming a sizable acreage of land, then the attraction of wildlife can be accomplished in an easier way than planting for them. You simply leave strips of crops unharvested around the boundaries of your farm, especially those bordering on wooded areas. Cover for wild creatures is most important. They are reluctant, and with good reason, to come out into unprotected fields. Millet and sorghum grains are invaluable as plantings for game animals and birds. They are also good for northern areas.

On banks and runs where there is a chance of water and rain washing away the soil, the sowing of either crown vetch or bird's-foot trefoil will do much to bind the soil and prevent erosion, as well as furnish food for many birds and animals.

Seedling hemlocks planted close together in rows will grow very rapidly to form perfect covers and nesting sites, as well as winter browse for deer.

Birches and willows, as well as other species of fast-growing trees, planted at the water's edge around your pond may very well encourage a beaver to make your land his home. This is even more likely if a small stream feeds your pond. However, make certain that by encouraging beavers, you are not starting something which will cause damage to your property. A beaver dam can cause water backups which will flood out many good farm acres if beavers are permitted full freedom to build their huts. They can be a curse as well as a blessing, so you should investigate carefully just what the water will cover and how far it will back up before allowing a beaver to dam off the flow.

Winter is a hard time for many animals, especially if it is a long and severe one. Small animals are kept from their normal food supply by the deep snow, or by ice crusts formed on the top so hard and thick that they cannot penetrate them. Deer cannot dig down to their browse, and are reduced to eating bark for sustenance, an ill-nourishing material at best for the hungry creatures. Common hay cannot be used by deer, something people often don't know. Some years ago, during an exceptionally long and severe winter, huge herds of deer were found to be on the verge of death from starvation, so the conservation department took loads of hay in helicopters, dropping the bales in the midst of the herds. All to no avail; the deer were later discovered dead in bunches, and upon examination of their stomachs it was found that the hay had been eaten all right, but the animals had not been able to digest it.

Subsequent inquiries showed that the cellulose content of hay cannot be assimilated by deer, because these animals lack protozoans in their intestinal system which can digest cellulose. They can, however, eat alfalfa, or other leguminous material.

So you should not put out hay for the deer during winter, but other acceptable foods instead. If alfalfa is not available, slender branches of trees, twigs with winter buds, and similar substances can be gathered and placed where the deer can find them. Some grain may also be supplied in feeding stations sheltered from wind and rain. Other animals will also help themselves, but that should not be the cause of too much worry.

I constantly hear the complaints of persons who feed birds. They say they cannot keep the feeders full because the squirrels take so much and scatter the rest. Other say that they want to feed the cardinals and the thrushes, but do not want the starlings, grackles, cowbirds, or bluejays to get any. Well, my opinion is that if you want to feed wildlife you simply do so. How anyone can say that a bluejay is not a part of wildlife is beyond me. The fact that bluejays are belligerent to other birds at times is beside the point. Nearly every living creature is belligerent to other creatures at one time or another, and especially when feeding. Animals completely lack what we call a moral sense. When they have young, they will feed the babies before themselves as a general rule, but at all other times the biggest and strongest gets the food first.

Also, when feeding birds you will notice that when plenty of food is available, such large birds as bluejays, cardinals, grackles, starlings, and others do not persistently persecute the smaller species, but feed right alongside them with perhaps an occasional peck if one of the others gets a bit too close.

As for squirrels scattering feed from a feeder—yes, they do so. But where's the damage? The birds pick seed off the ground, or off the snow, for that matter, as readily as they take it from the feeder, and as a matter of fact, many of the birds, being ground feeders, prefer their seed on the ground, so the squirrels are performing a service rather than a disservice.

After feeding birds for more than ten consecutive years on our place in the country, we have come to realize that all the different species deserve the same treatment, and no single kind of creature should be excluded from the dining room just because of its behavioral life. If this were not so, I should certainly try to do everything in my power to see that shrikes were driven from the face of the earth, let alone my own feeding stations. I do not like shrikes because of the things they do. They feed upon insects, but they also fly down, capture, and kill other birds. This is not the thing that condemns them in my thoughts, however. It is their gruesome habit of taking young birds in their beaks and impaling them on thorns, where they remain in a kind of storage until the shrike is once more hungry. The same process is followed with caterpillars and other large insects, and any thorn bush or hawthorn tree may have at any given time several victims stuck fast to the thorns, making a kind of horrible pantry for these birds.

I know that I am being unfair and foolish about it, but this is the way a shrike affects me. I suppose I would not have that strong a feeling about them if I had not seen one run down a meadowlark on a sunny warm afternoon. The flight aerobatics were a wonder to behold. The lark performed like an aviator in a dogfight in the clouds, and it was the relentless pursuit of the shrike that gave me the chill up my spine. I, on the sidelines, so to speak, could see that none of the lark's superb flight ability was going to do it any good, and that it was only a matter of time before it would fall victim to its savage pursuer.

And yet "savage" is not fair, either, because the shrike was merely doggedly hunting its prey for its own survival. Viciousness was not a factor.

Chapter
4

Animal Diets
and Habits

I think it might be a good idea to describe some of the animals seen around suburban and rural homes in this country and to list some of the things in their regular diet. Then when little Johnny wanders home with a "lost" animal, at least you will have an idea what to feed it.

However, please realize that the emphasis in this book is not on keeping these animals prisoner, but rather on liberating them if caught, and on observing them around your home without molesting them. The feeding should be done outside to attract them, rather than to try to capture them. In time, if you do feed the animals the kinds of foods they like and require, you will find a veritable menagerie of creatures coming to visit you, and becoming tame enough even to take food from your hands at times.

Mammals

Shrews, Moles

Forget them. They require their own weight or more in insects and vegetable matter each day. Without this, they will die within a few hours, literally of starvation. Their metabolic rate is astonishing, and the pulse rate is over 1,200 per minute!

Mice

The common field mouse in the East is the deer mouse, or white-footed mouse. Deer mice eat anything in the way of insects, vegetation, fruits, baby birds, and, in hard times, tree bark and each other. Very neat, clean little animals. Brown on top and snow-white beneath. Come in house mainly in the wintertime. Can be destructive in houses.

Raccoons

These "bandits" hardly need description, since almost everyone knows what a raccoon looks like, with its grayish fur and the black mask over the eyes. They feed on insects, fish and other aquatic life, small animals, fruits, and vegetables. They may raid your cornfield at harvesttime and will sometimes eat a chicken, but more than pay for it in the number of mice and rats they eat throughout the year. They are very inquisitive, and, when young, are easily tamed. Fierce fighters when cornered, they can overpower and kill a large dog if necessary.

Skunks

These lazy black-and-white creatures have a perfect defense mechanism, although they do not necessarily use it at all times. In fact, you really have to force a skunk to let go with its musk. Do not be misled into believing the old tale that a skunk cannot spray you if held by the tail, or in any other position. It can and will, and is not to be blamed if you treat it that way. Skunks give a sort of warning when they are about to let go. The final sign is stamping their front feet. When they begin to stamp, you begin to run! Their food consists of insects for more than half their diet. Fruits, grains, vegetables, and mice make up the bulk of the remainder. Some birds are eaten, as well as other small animals. They have been known to eat a chicken now and then, but this is unusual. They perform an extremely valuable service in eating grubs, potato beetle larvae, and other insects injurious to crops and gardens. The striped skunk is found over the entire United States. The spotted skunk is not found on the Eastern seaboard, in the Great Lakes states, or in Montana.

Otters

These fun-loving animals are usually found around water, and if you have a lake, pond, or stream on your property there might just be an otter or two there as well. They are found all over the country except in the

The otter swims almost as well as the fish that make up its diet. They inhabit streams and ponds. (Photo: U.S. Forest Service)

Southwest. They grow to be pretty big animals, five feet long, with a heavy foot-long tail. Their food is mainly fish, but they will eat birds and other animals, and sometimes poultry. They make good pets, but should not be kept in captivity, because they range widely and require a lot of water for their well-being.

Weasels, Ferrets

While ferrets have a more limited range, weasels are found nearly all over the country. Often their nests are dug up during road making, or in digging for building foundations. When taken young, they become quite tame. Ferrets are used extensively in Europe and occasionally in this country to hunt rabbits and rats. The ferrets go right down the burrows to run their prey out. Their food is primarily small ani-

Weasels are wonderful little animals and are not at all mean when taken young.

mals like rabbits, rats, mice, birds, and sometimes poultry if they are not protected where weasels are known to live. Weasels perform a very great service to mankind in the killing of pest animals such as rats.

Minks are extremely irritable; their sharp teeth can do a lot of damage to a poking finger.

Minks

While wild mink are to be seen once in a while, especially near wooded areas, this very valuable animal is more often found in captivity, where it is raised by the thousands to provide fur for garments. The food of these creatures is rats, mice, fish, and poultry, as well as birds.

Ermine

This animal is seen only in the winter. It is pure white, with a black tip on the tail. At other seasons of the year, the fur is dark and the animal is one of the weasels. They range extensively throughout the country. Their diet is like that of other weasels, but they are marvelous rat killers and should be encouraged to stay around farms and farm buildings.

Foxes

The smaller red fox is more commonly seen than the larger gray fox. Both of them will steal a chicken out of your run unless the pen is well secured. Both animals range nearly everywhere in this country. The red fox is the greatest killer of mice known. It accounts for millions of these pests each year. Foxes also eat fruit and vegetables, and other small animals like squirrels and chipmunks, birds, etc., but they more than pay their way as mousers.

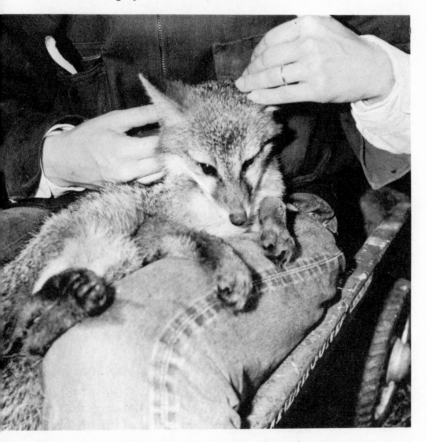

Foxes are beautiful animals and can become quite tame.

Wolves

Although the wolf has become nearly extinct in the United States, except for small packs in some areas where the animal is finally protected, still dwellers in woods areas, especially in Wisconsin and Michigan, may see a wolf or two at one time or other. They do not come to a house very often, but they are seen prowling at the edges of wooded places. Wolves will eat almost any animal, and they are capable of killing an animal as large as a moose. Best give them a wide berth if you see one. There is a pack on Isle Royale in Lake Superior.

Coyotes

A smaller version of the wolf, coyotes are usually heard at night rather than seen. Sometimes an animal near starvation will prowl the grounds of a home in the West and Southwest, but these animals are seldom seen in the eastern part of the country. While the coyote is an excellent ratter, it also takes rabbits, sheep and goats, poultry, and any other creature it can overpower. It also eats a lot of carrion. The howling of a coyote is unmistakable when once you hear it, and it is a lonesome and awe-inspiring call in the dead of the night.

Lynxes

From New York in a band across the upper part of the country one is quite apt to see a lynx now and then. In the more populated areas the lynx has abandoned its range, but people living at the borders of forest lands may very well run across them. The lynx is a large

In the dim early morning one day, this female cougar came to loll on our front porch. I took the photograph through the window.

cat, reaching a length of three feet. The main part of the diet is rats, mice, small rodents of other species, and carrion, as well as game birds and rabbits. It probably eats some vegetable matter too. Baby lynx can be tamed, but it is far better to leave this animal to its wild habitat. When it matures, there is the good possibility that it will turn on its captors.

Bobcats, Wildcats

The bobcat is similar to the lynx and feeds on the same diet. It is also a large animal, reaching the size of a lynx or even larger. The ears are pointed, but not as long or as sharp as those of the lynx. Except for the east-central states, the bobcat ranges all over the United States. It will flee rather than attack a person unless it is cornered or its young are threatened.

Mountain Lions, Cougars, Pumas, Painters

These are different names for the same animal. The mountain lion is one of the most magnificent animals on this continent, and it should not be exterminated, as now seems to be the trend. It very rarely attacks man, but will kill and eat sheep, goats, cattle and horses, deer, and other animals. It eats a small quantity of vegetable matter at times. As with other animals of this type, it is not a good practice to try to tame one. They are too dangerous when adult, because of their great strength and size, even if they are not vicious.

Woodchucks, Groundhogs, Marmots

Who has not seen one of these rough-coated brown animals sitting erect on the highway shoulder, contentedly munching the vegetation? Around the home in the country, the woodchuck can be a real nuisance because of its fondness for tomatoes. A woodchuck will go through an entire tomato patch, taking a bite out of each tomato, instead of consuming one and leaving the rest. Fences will not keep them out unless the bottoms of the wires are buried about two feet underground, because woodchucks are wonderful burrowers and can easily dig their way under an ordinary fence. Other than their depredations in your gardens, the animals are harmless. They will not try to attack you, but can bite if cornered and attacked. They live in burrows dug in dry soil in fields or woods. They are edible, but the meat is strong, stringy, and tough.

The chubby woodchuck can be a garden pest, but it is otherwise a harmless and entertaining neighbor.

Chipmunks

These attractive little squirrel-type animals live in burrows, generally in among rocks. They are active and inquisitive, and are death to garden bulbs unless you plant them under a screen as described in Chapter 2. The little animals also invade attics and cellars occasionally. Their food consists of insects, grubs, birds, other small animals such as moles and voles, nuts, fruits, vegetables, and, of course, your prize tulip bulbs. When taken as babies, they become very tame, and make good pets.

This self-confident gray squirrel makes his home in New York's Central Park. (Photo: Bob Elman)

The flying squirrel's enormous eyes give it good night vision. They make delightful pets.

Squirrels

Gray squirrels are one of the very few animals which have adapted themselves to living around people, and to living in cities. There is practically no city in the United States which does not have its population of

59

gray squirrels, either in the parks or in the city streets, where they nest in the trees and find food as best they can. Red squirrels are smaller than gray squirrels. They are most apt to be found in coniferous woodland—and, all too often, in your attic. Squirrels are beautiful animals to begin with, and this probably has a lot to do with their being tolerated by man, who usually feeds them when they appear. The diet of squirrels is mainly vegetable matter, nuts, and fruits, but they also eat some insects and some meat. When young, gray squirrels are very tame, and can be picked up and handled with impunity. They are edible, and considered excellent eating by some people.

Flying Squirrels

This nocturnal animal is rarely seen by man, although it is plentiful and is a main food source for owls and other predators. It is a completely endearing little creature and becomes very tame and affectionate in captivity. Fruits, nuts, and an insect or two constitute the diet of flying squirrels. They are active all year, but only at night. They glide from tree to tree and can cover short distances on the ground with surprising speed.

Coypus, Nutrias

While this animal is actually a South American species, indigenous to Peru and Chile, it has become established in our Southern states through escapees to the Florida swamps. It was brought into this country to be reared as a fur animal. It is primarily an aquatic animal, and its diet consists mainly of aquatic plants, roots, and seeds. While still confined to a few Southern states, this animal is looked upon as a possible pest, because of the rapidity with which it multiplies. It is now hunted in the wild for its fur. At times, especially in Florida and Mississippi, the coypu has been seen in gardens around houses, where, even though it is a large animal, it is harmless, except for possible damage to the plants.

Beavers

Unless you have a stream running through your property, you are not apt to be bothered with beavers. Perhaps "bothered" is not quite the correct term. Beavers make dams across small streams, to create a pond in which they can build their rather extensive lodges. The damming of the stream can, and often does, flood land that you may otherwise want to use. An orchard can be flooded out, or a garden area, and once beavers have decided that this is where they are going to live, even the destruction of their dam will not help much, because they will simply rebuild it as fast as you destroy it. Since the diet of beavers is almost exclusively bark and the wood of soft trees, they do not directly damage gardens, but they can flood them and destroy trees you wish to keep. Live-trapping them and removing them to another location is about the best way to cope with these interesting animals. On the other hand, if you can accept their encroachment philosophically, you will benefit by having a corps of excellent engineers construct a beautiful natural pond for you, which can, and usually does, enhance the value of any property. (However, beaver ponds are usually unsuitable for swimming because of the quantities of saplings and branches the beavers bring into them.)

Porcupines

The porcupine is a stupid animal, and one that at first thought seems to have no redeeming features. However, it is of some value. First of all they are good to eat, tasting something like pork. They are not a menace to human beings, being slow and placid, but they present a real problem to dogs, because these foolish beasts cannot seem to learn to keep their snoots away from the animated pincushions. About the only damage porcupines are apt to do around the house is destroy your evergreen plants. They are fond of the foliage of these kinds of shrubs. They also like salt, and can be attracted to the yard by putting out a salt block or two. They are crepuscular, active for the most part at dusk and at dawn. They are inordinately fond of chocolate, and if one does come into your yard, you will make a fast friend of it if you offer it a Hershey bar.

Porcupines love chocolate. While not exactly cuddly, they do little damage except to inquisitive dogs.

Rabbits

These animals are for the most part pests rather than welcome visitors. They seem to know exactly the day your bulb flowers send the first tender shoots out of the ground, and they are right there to mow them to the ground line. Nothing is safe in a garden from these wiggle-nosed creatures. In the East we have the cottontail, and in the West the jackrabbit is common. They are good eating, but there is danger in handling wild rabbits because they carry tularemia, which is fatal to human beings. Unless the animal is handled there is no danger of contracting the disease, however.

Deer

In the East the white-tailed deer are common, and in the West, both mule deer and whitetails are encountered. A deer may come regularly to your yard, and become so tame as to take food from your hand. These creatures love apples, and will raid orchards whenever they have a chance. They can be attracted by a salt lick, but be sure to place the salt block where it will not leach into the soil around the roots of trees that you want to protect. Many trees, particularly evergreens, are very sensitive to salt.

Armadillos

In the southern part of this country armadillos abound, and, secure in their armor, they often come right into your yard looking for their main source of food—ants. The armadillo is primarily an anteater, and as such performs a valuable service to mankind, in helping to keep these sometimes annoying insects in check. Except for the steel-hard claws, the armadil-

Cottontails are no friend to the gardener, but they are fun to watch and are a very important part of the food chain in woodland areas. (Photo: Bob Elman)

lo is harmless. They become tame if taken when young. One person I know has kept an armadillo for a few years that she obtained on a vacation trip to Mexico when it was small enough to sleep in an old teacup. She puts it out to graze on her lawn, where it spends all its time digging up grubs, cutworms, earth-worms, and harmful beetle larvae which compose much of its diet in captivity.

Insects

Scorpions

In the southern half of the United States, several species of scorpions live. Altogether there are about twenty-five species of this interesting arachnid in this country. Contrary to popular stories, the scorpion does not sting itself and commit suicide when trapped. It is impervious to its own venom. Scorpions are likely to be found in shoes, clinging in clothing, and in dark crevices. They prefer dry locations and a warm climate. Their sting is not fatal to adults, but it is possible that a child could be killed by one. Knock out shoes and shake out your clothing before donning it if you live in "scorpion country" as a safe precaution against being stung.

Tarantulas, Bird Spiders

Some species of this wonderful arachnid are as large as a saucer, counting their eight legs. Both bodies and legs are furred. There are brown species and black ones, and the species in this country are not venomous, although you may hear fantastic stories to the contrary. Their bite is very painful, however. Large tarantulas may catch and kill birds. I once witnessed a brown tarantula kill and devour a large lizard, leaving the cleanly picked skeleton as the only evidence of its feast. They are mostly active at night, and it is not a good practice to go barefoot on the lawn after dark. Tarantulas may be kept in captivity and live contentedly for a long time. It is difficult to get them to bite a person.

Daddy Longlegs, Harvestmen

Although these creatures look like attenuated spiders, they really are a giant mite. They do not point in the direction of cows, as is commonly told to credulous people. They feed on small insects and decaying vegetable matter, and are completely harmless to people.

Black Widow Spiders, Hour-Glass Spiders

This arachnid has an exaggerated reputation, but still it should be treated with caution. The bite will not kill a healthy adult, but it could possibly kill a child. The spider can be recognized by its shiny black body, and by the red or orange mark on its abdomen, shaped like an hourglass. It inhabits dark, damp areas such as cellars, corners of rotten wooden boxes, outhouses, and similar locations. It will not bite without provocation.

All Other Spiders

Garden spiders, house spiders, and the like need not be feared. They have no venom for the most part, they are almost completely reluctant to bite, and many of them cannot even bite a human being to begin with. They perform a very great service in the house of snaring mosquitoes and other flying insects which would otherwise make your life miserable. Cherish the house spider, and do not swat every one you see.

Dobsonflies

These large winged creatures—the wingspread is five inches—congregate around yard lights and street lights in masses of thousands. The larval form is called a hellgrammite, and is valued as a fishing bait. Both the larva and the adult have powerful jaws and can give you a severe nip. Otherwise they are harmless.

Dragonflies, Damselflies, Darning Needles

These beautiful insects can often be seen on warm sunny afternoons, hovering over any spot of water,

Dragonflies are large and dart about fearlessly, and consequently many people fear them. Actually they are a most beautiful insect and entirely harmless.

67

even over a play pool or pail. One of the unfounded tales spread about them is that they sew your eyelids shut, or sew your lips shut. This is pure balderdash. They are completely harmless, and are one of the very best killers of mosquitoes and flying pests we have. You should do everything you can to protect these useful creatures.

Reptiles and Amphibians

Salamanders

There are many species of salamander in the United States. All are harmless. Often you will turn one up when digging in your garden. They live under rocks, boards, or anything that remains on the ground long enough to permit moisture to collect underneath. They feed on worms, grubs, insects, small animals, frogs, etc. They are valuable in gardens because they clean out grubs which would be injurious to plants. Some of the salamanders live for twenty or twenty-five years, and are often used to decorate moist terrariums. Mealworms, worms, grubs, and other insects dropped into the terrarium will keep salamanders in good health. They soon learn to come to the spot where you drop in the food to take it as soon as it is offered. Their skin must be kept moist at all times or they will perish.

Toads

The common toad is the prime food of the hog-nosed snake, as well as of other animals. Toads do not give you warts, regardless of the stories you may have been told about them. Toads live on insects, and in the evening may be seen squatting under a light, or even in the light shining out a window, waiting for insects to be attracted to it and drop to the ground. Toads should be protected and encouraged to live in your garden.

Snakes

Since I have devoted a whole chapter in this book to the discussion of reptiles and amphibians, I won't go any further into it at this time, except to repeat that any snake you see around your home should be left strictly alone to perform its invaluable service to you in catching rats, mice, and other varmints that would otherwise find haven around the place. Unless your property is wooded and wild, you will not see any copperheads or rattlesnakes around. Unless you live in the Deep South, you will not come across coral snakes, and even if you do live there, you will have to dig or plow them up to see them. Unless there is a lot of water on your property, water moccasins are not a problem. They won't be a problem even if they are there in your pond or stream. So let us all try to change our philosophy about the lowly serpent, and give it the respect and appreciation it deserves.

Lizards, Skinks

The same thing goes for lizards and skinks as for snakes. They are valuable animals, interesting to watch, and harmless to people. They help keep the insect population in check, and some of the larger ones even eat rats and mice.

69

Turtles

These, too, should be protected. Some species are fond of nibbling a leaf of lettuce in the garden, but they eat very little—in comparison with a rabbit or woodchuck, for example—and the other things they eat, such as snails and grubs, more than pay for the leaf. They are also fond of mushrooms and toadstools. Pay no attention to the story that if a turtle eats a mushroom, that mushroom is good for you to eat too. Turtles can eat mushrooms that are deadly to human beings with impunity, so this tale is completely unfounded. I might add here that squirrels also eat poisonous mushrooms.

Birds

For some reason or other people do not fear birds as they do mammals and reptiles. Perhaps this is because birds are so pretty as a rule, and because birds take off at their first sight of man. I have already cautioned you not to feed birds unless you continue to do so the entire year through. At the woods edge or among thick trees, scattered chicken scratch or cracked corn may attract partridge. These are impressive birds which sound like a helicopter when they take wing. Pheasant may also come to such a handout. If you keep chickens and live in the woods, hawks and owls may be a problem. Also, many people raise gamebirds as a hobby or a side business, and here they face a real problem, that of the great horned owl. Quail and other game birds have the habit of flying straight up in the air when frightened. When they are reared in pens, you must have a screen on the top as well as all

Young rough-legged hawks, about ready to leave the nest.

around. At night, owls will come and take position in a tree above the pen, then dive at the pen with a hoot. In a panic the birds will fly up against the top of the screen, sticking their heads through the mesh, where the owl snips them off as fast as they appear, and the headless bodies of the birds fall to the ground. For this reason you should have a double screen on the tops of

The great horned owl is as much a predator as the hawks. This nearly tame one sits on our back fence all day, waiting for a handout.

your pens, with about a six-inch space between the two. The danger of losing poultry to hawks is a lot less than people might believe. I know some farmers—and people who are not farmers, for that matter—who say that every hawk which flies will kill their chickens. Even the little kestrel, called the sparrow hawk, is not immune from this accusation. Once in a while a hawk will take a chicken if it is out in a field and is easy prey. I know of no instance where hawks have come down into a coop in the yard. Perhaps sometimes they do, but I am inclined to give the hawk the benefit of the doubt and place the blame on a 'possum or other animal.

Possibly you will have some creature visit you that I have not listed here. But I sincerely hope that you have learned from these pages that you really have nothing to fear from these creatures, and that you have a lot to learn from them.

So, when you go out in the evening to dump the garbage and are met with two bright eyes shining in the dusk, enjoy. Feel honored that the little fellow has so overcome his fear of *you* that he has approached closely enough for you to see him.

Chapter
5

Reptiles
and Amphibians

There's a snake! *Kill it!*

What unfortunate philosophy causes such an instant reaction in 99 out of 100 people when they see a snake gliding through the grasses? Perhaps, the Bible is largely to blame for this, since when the narrator who wrote Genesis picked an animal to blame for man's falling from grace, he picked the serpent. Countless millions of these poor creatures were thus needlessly condemned to death, their race despised, and their very name a cause for a shudder of revulsion.

Of all the animals living on the entire planet—more than a million different species—the snake is without question the most maligned, the most persecuted, and the most feared. Why? The answers to that question are as varied as the number of people I ask it of.

"Because snakes are evil." What is evil about a snake? Let us analyze that statement. The definition of "evil" according to the second edition of *Webster's New International Dictionary* is as follows:

EVIL: 1. Having qualities tending to injury and mischief; mischievous; not good; worthless; poor.

2. Having or exhibiting bad moral qualities; morally corrupt; wicked.

3. Producing or threatening sorrow, distress, or calamity; unpropitious; calamitous.

4. Arising from bad character, actual or imputed.

5. Defective; unsatisfactory.

6. Unsound, diseased; also unwholesome.

7. Offensive; repulsive; malignant, highly unpleasant.

These are the meanings given by an accepted authority. With only one exception, no definition is applicable to snakes. That exception is definition number 7, and even that is subject to much editing. First of all, the fear of snakes—let me correct that to say the fear of any living creature—is an unnatural emotion. The human animal is born, perhaps, with a fear of falling, but that is all. *Every other fear that a person lives with has to be taught to him by someone who himself was taught that fear.* A small child, introduced to a snake for the first time, will happily try to play with it. One can offer any kind of harmless snake to him—garter snake, bull snake, king snake—name it, and there will not be the slightest hesitation on the part of the child to play with it, to handle it, and to cuddle it. There is no feeling of repulsion, of offensiveness, of malignancy, or anything other than interest in the animal because it is alive. The exact same emotion will be displayed if you hand the child a rattlesnake or a cobra, either of which is capable of

The garter snake, one of the most common and most beautiful of North American snakes, is utterly harmless and easily tamed—like most other snakes. (Photo: Bob Elman)

killing the child with a single bite.

Doesn't this indicate that all this business of snakes being repulsive and terrifying is an unfounded and induced emotion on the part of the average human being? It does to me.

As a matter of fact, there is nothing repulsive about snakes. To the contrary, some of them are among the most beautiful animals we have on earth. Most of them are also among the most useful animals. There is no question but that some of the species are dangerous—a few dangerous in the extreme. These should be steered clear of with a passion, but certainly not slaughtered on sight *because they are snakes.*

In the United States we have but four species of snake which carry venom: the rattlesnake, the coral snake, the water moccasin, and the copperhead. Let us take a closer look at these four creatures. First, the rattlesnake. There are a number of different kinds of

If this photograph makes you shudder, you have been brainwashed. My young son is showing a quite proper interest in a very elegant specimen of Marcy's snake.

rattlesnake, living in different locations, from the small desert sidewinder to the truly fearsome and very dangerous timber rattler, living in the forest regions of the South, East, and other areas of the country.

If and when you come upon such a snake, it will warn you. Let me say right at the beginning of this discussion that snakes *do not* attack people, jumping

The timber rattlesnake is truly dangerous—but it gives fair warning, and is no hazard to anyone with common sense. (Photo: courtesy R. D. Bahret)

out at them unaware, striking with all their fierce venom intent only upon killing you. This is one of the old wives' tales about these most maligned creatures.

When you come upon a rattlesnake in its natural habitat, it will first try to glide away unseen by you, and you will be entirely unaware that you were even near a rattlesnake. If, however, you move into a position which cuts off the escape route of the animal, it will coil up, extend its tail from the center of the coil, and rattle vigorously. You will hear the rattle, unless you happen to be deaf. A deaf person should never travel in rattlesnake country without accompaniment by a person with good hearing.

The rattle of a rattlesnake is not—contrary to popular belief—an offensive gesture, threatening you with sudden death, but a purely defensive measure. The snake is advertising its presence to what, to it, is a threat of predation. It is noisily proclaiming to all and sundry: Here am I; I am capable of defending myself; do not push me into using my defense; just leave me alone.

All you have to do on hearing a rattlesnake rattle is stand still. Look around you, and you will soon locate the animal, coiled, ready to strike if you provoke it. Make no move, and soon the snake will gradually uncoil, to slip away quietly to safety. The danger is past. There never is any *real* danger—provided you leave the creature alone.

A person can thread his way with impunity through a veritable nest of rattlesnakes, and as long as he does not approach closely enough to alarm any particular individual, he will not be attacked. A rattlesnake can strike for a distance about equal to a third or a half of its length. If you are not very good at judging short distances accurately, then play safe and stay 8 or 10 feet away from each snake. No problem. Very seldom do you find a rattlesnake crawling right about your home. If you have property with wide expanses and rocky places, that is where they will most likely be found, and even then, you won't see them very often.

Copperheads are a little different. They like dark, damp places like piles of dead leaves, or an old log in forest locations. Copperheads will lie curled up and make no attempt to attack you if you pass by. If you step on them, however, or step so close to them that they think you are about to attack, they will strike. The usual bite from a copperhead results from stepping over an old log before looking where you are putting your foot.

The bite of a copperhead, while venomous, still is not a dangerous affair. True, you will be sick for a while, a day or so, and the site of the punctures will swell, somewhat painfully, but unless you are really in very poor health or have such an uncontrollable fear of a snake that you go completely out of control the bite is not serious. I have been bitten on the ankle by a copperhead under just the conditions described, and the result was a little pain and nausea for a day, accompanied by a swelling that made it necessary to go without my shoe for a couple of days longer. Copperheads are likely to be encountered in brushy or woodsy areas. Just watch where you step, or, if you turn over logs or large stones, do so with caution, looking carefully as you lift the object. Again, there is no danger of attack from a copperhead if you leave it alone.

Coral snakes live in the warmer sections of the South, and are primarily a subterranean snake, coming out of their burrows only if they are rained out or plowed up. They will first make a desperate attempt to escape you, trying to bite only if you persist in molesting them. They are a small snake, and very beautifully colored, but their mouth is small and they have almost to be encouraged to bite you to do it successfully. Their venom is the most dangerous of our poisonous snakes, being the same kind of venom as a cobra. A little goes a long way with a coral-snake bite, and they should be treated with extreme caution.

The water moccasin lives, as its name implies, in or near the water—on the banks of streams, ponds, or lakes and in swampy places. The bite of a moccasin is not necessarily fatal, although there are some recorded deaths from the venom. It is, though, a nasty affair, and very painful. The water moccasin is an ugly snake, colored a dark brown, mottled a bit. It is a fat, short, stumpy snake, with a rough hide and a large head. When it opens its mouth in warning, or to strike, the inside is clear white and pudgy. From this

The copperhead is also venomous, and something of a hazard because it lies quiet and almost invisible on dead leaves or rotting logs. But the bite is rarely deadly. (Photo: courtesy R. D. Bahret)

the animal takes its popular name of cottonmouth. It is easy to identify this snake from the inside of its mouth, and easy not to mistake other snakes for water moccasins, because no other snake has the white fluffy mouth that this one has. Upon encountering a moccasin, you merely have to walk away from it. It will more than likely be on its own way in a different direction from yours.

Other than these four kinds of snakes, we have no venomous species in our country.

We do have, however, many species that are commonly called every name under the sun, most of the names indicating varying degrees of malignancy and poisonous ability. One such is the gentle, innocuous hognose snake or hog-nosed viper. The name "hog-nosed viper" is most unfortunate, because, especially in Africa, vipers are among the deadliest and most dangerous snakes in the world. The name is misleading; the snake we have here is really incapable of doing any harm. It is, in fact, the clown of the snake family. It is also called the spreading adder, hissing adder, and several other names equally misleading and fear-provoking to the uninitiated.

Hognose snakes feed on toads—the common garden variety of toad. Some will also eat a frog or other amphibian, but toads are the preferred food. When discovered the first thing the hognose snake will do is to raise its head a bit and spread a wide hood, exactly like a cobra. It will weave its hood back and forth, hoping to instill enough terror in its annoyer to end the molestation.

If, however, the predator, be it man or another animal, keeps its courage and persists in its "attack" the snake goes into phase two of its defense. It coils like a rattlesnake, with the tail erect in the center, and the head in the well-known S-curve ready to strike down its mortal enemy with its deadly bite, and proceeds to rattle ominously. The only thing wrong with all that is that the snake has no rattles, and the tail merely vibrates silently in the air. If the snake happens to be sitting on a pile of dead leaves and the tail is touching the leaves, there will be a slight rustle, but that is all. While phases one and two are in progress, the "deadly" creature is also hissing like a locomotive letting off steam. It hisses both inhaling and exhaling, so it produces a steady volume of sound.

When phase two also fails there is still phase three. Phase three is really a humdinger. Since the predator evidently fears neither cobras or rattlesnakes, there is but one thing left to do. Who would want a dead snake? Dead snakes are worthless to almost anyone. So our specimen dies. One thing first, though. The snake has to have a reason to die, so it throws a fit. It goes into "convulsions," writhing about and thrashing its short stumpy body around on the ground, opening

Blue racers mating. A colony of these mouse-eating snakes inhabit a rock pit on my property and keep my house free of mice.

its mouth and sticking out its tongue to drag in the dust. When it decides you have been properly impressed by its fatal seizure, it will come to rest—on its back, tongue still protruding and dusty—and expire. You can pick it up and hang it over a branch, and nothing will happen. After all, a dead snake would just hang there.

Turn your back, however, and stand still. Then suddenly snap around to look at the snake again. It will be slowly turning over on its tummy to crawl to safety, but immediately on your looking at it will snap right back on its back again. Out comes the tongue, and it is again dead. By this time, if you aren't laughing so hard you can't manage it, you can pick it up and stuff it in your pocket to take home as a pet.

Hognose snakes make wonderful pets, if you keep them supplied with toads. With a nice fat toad every other day or every few days at the least, it will live contentedly and long in captivity. It will provide amusement with its bag of tricks—but for a short time only. The trouble is that it will become tame very

83

fast, will lose its fear of you, and will no longer need to go through its defense mechanisms.

Every once in a while you may find a tiny snake no larger than a big night-crawler worm. This is the little subterranean blind snake. It has no eyes—or at best, only vestigial eyes, covered with membranes. They are called worm snakes, and, indeed, they do resemble worms, except they are not slimy and moist like worms, but dry and smooth like other true snakes. When you find one of them in your yard, usually toward evening, put it back and let it go its way. It is busy helping you as hard as it can, by searching out and devouring ant and termite grubs and larvae, as well as the mature insects.

In some parts of the country another small brown snake is so abundant that it seems to be found everywhere you turn, hiding under anything lying on the ground. These are the DeKay's snakes, of which there are many subspecies. They have all been grouped together and called little brown snakes. These too are your helpers, hunting beetle grubs, slugs, earthworms, and insects like crickets and grasshoppers.

Little brown snakes are found even in large cities. They manage to survive in a vacant lot, a park, or almost anywhere there is a plot of ground large enough to support a population of the insects on which they feed. Central Park, in the heart of teeming New York City, has a very large population of little brown snakes.

There are several species of snakes which are often seen around the house in the country. All of them are very beneficial to mankind, feeding on rats, mice, insects, and harmful creatures in general. None of them are dangerous, and none of them should be killed. Rather they should be encouraged, although I cannot tell you just how to go about encouraging a snake to take up its abode near you. I did liberate three female and two male Western garter snakes on my own property about six years ago, and we see them each year. They not only have decided to remain here, but a couple of years ago we found several baby snakes, so they obviously have mated and had at least one litter of young. Of course, some time in the distant future some scientist is going to come across one of these Western visitors, two thousand and more miles off its range, and he will be very puzzled. I will probably be long gone from this life and he will have no explanation of how they came to be living in Saugerties, N.Y., when they are supposed to be found in California.

In the eastern part of the country, the most commonly seen snakes will be the rat snakes, corn snake, milk snake, bull snake, and similar species. All of the species mentioned are of inestimable value, feeding on rats and mice. Farmers would be hard put to cope with the rodent population if it were not for the assistance of these despised creatures. It is some help that now farmers are more aware of the value of the snakes around their barns and leave them alone instead of running the harrow over them on sight.

The stories about snakes are almost beyond belief. Milk snakes, for example, acquired their name because they are supposed to suck the milk from cows, leaving the cow barren and dry. Actually, the reason milk snakes are always crawling around the cow barns is that barns are where the rats and mice gather to feed and spread their diseases, and the milk snake feeds on these rodents. They do *not* drink milk, either from the cow or any other way.

The whipsnake, which is named because it is long

and thin like a whip, does not use its tail to lash you to ribbons with, nor does it attack people in any other way. The hoopsnake, so feared in the South, does not take its tail in its mouth, forming a hoop to roll after you in deadly pursuit. The hoopsnake is as harmless as the hognose snake. The glass snake does not break into little pieces when you pick it up, to rejoin its length after sundown. In fact, the glass snake is not even a snake at all. It is a legless lizard, and like most all lizards, it has the ability to shed its tail if caught. Lizards' tails are so constructed that if the creature is caught and held by the tail, it can snap off the body of the animal. As soon as this happens, nerves in the tail cause it to writhe about frantically, capturing the attention of the predator while the now tailless lizard quietly scurries to safety, only to grow a new, somewhat stumpier tail in a short time.

In the South and the West, king snakes may often be seen around the home. These are especially valuable guests, because, besides feeding on rats and mice, they will kill and eat poisonous snakes like rattlesnakes, water moccasins, and copperheads, performing a kind of double service to the race which holds them in such contempt and slaughters them in such prodigious numbers.

And so, instead of being creatures that should be killed on sight, or run from screaming in fear, snakes should be given the consideration due to them as valued animals. They more than pay their way in the ecosystem of which they are a part. I would venture to say that mankind would find it difficult if not impossible to exist if it were not for the snakes. These maligned and persecuted animals are responsible for the extermination of millions of rats and mice every year. Farms—yes, and homes too—would soon be

Holbrook's king snake, like other king snakes, is very gentle and will not bite. They are better mousers than cats—and will also eat poisonous snakes!

overrun with the rodent hordes were it not for the diligent and persistent races of snakes.

Besides snakes, there are a few other reptiles and amphibians which are commonly seen about the home in rural areas. Several species of lizard may be observed scurrying rapidly out of your sight. You may not even see them, but just hear the rustle of the leaves as they disappear to safety. No lizard in the United States is harmful, except the Gila monster, which is found in the arid Southwest. Even this one will not attack you, and can be dangerous only if you bully it so unmercifully that it finally, in desperation, tries to bite you.

Usually Gila monsters are sluggish and torpid. Make no mistake, however. The reason for this torpidity is cold. The animal can tolerate an enormous amount of heat, and is sluggish unless very warm.

The Florida king snake, a very pretty member of a valuable race of snakes.

When it is warm enough, a Gila monster can move so fast as to almost blur in your vision. They are useful animals and should not be killed.

Toads are very commonly seen in the garden and on the lawn. Under no circumstances should these be killed or molested, since each one accounts for literally hundreds of insects each night. Put on an outside light, and watch the toads gather in a circle beneath it, waiting for the insects to fly against the bulb and drop to the ground, where they are eagerly snapped up by the hungry little amphibians. Beetles, mosquitos, flies, ants—almost any insect that comes along is good food for these garden policemen.

In the Southwest, a very commonly seen animal is the horned "toad." This is not a toad at all, but a short-tailed lizard, and, again, one of the most beneficial of animals. The horned lizard feeds mainly on ants. One or more will take up a position on the side of an anthill, nose pointing to the opening, and wait for the active little insects to appear. As fast as the ants pop out of the opening, the lizards pop out their sticky

The collared lizard is a small relative of the iguana.

tongues to lap them up. A large horned lizard will eat several hundred ants a day, and a colony of them can clean out a large nest with no difficulty.

Horned lizards of some species have an odd defense mechanism. When frightened or attacked, these little creatures can expel a stream of blood from the inner corners of their eyes! They project this stream with great accuracy, and it must be confusing to a predator to be met with such a projectile rather than a mouthful of succulent lizard. I know it confuses humans encountering this trait for the first time. The blood is harmless, although messy and startling. It is merely a shock device that gains the lizard time to run for a hiding spot.

Most horned lizards have a ring of sharp spines encircling the back of the head. Some have spines on other parts of the body, and one species from California carries a veritable collar of long pointed spines. While they look fierce, they are in fact one of the most gentle of animals and never bite when handled. They are gathered and sold by the thousands by mail-order pet and animal dealers, and they die miserably by equal thousands because they are not given enough of their proper food or the right ecological conditions for survival. Ants—living ants—in large quantities must be fed them, and they must have a warm dry location, with sand or dusty soil under which to burrow.

Turtles come often to the yard or garden. They are looking for the soft, succulent slugs which devour the leaves of plants and vegetables. Turtles are innocuous creatures, with the exception of snapping turtles, which when adult are capable of taking off a finger when they are aroused. Snapping turtles have nasty dispositions, and seem always to be looking for a quarrel. They live only around water.

The most plentiful turtles in the Eastern section are the wood turtles, painted turtles, box turtles, and spotted turtles. The painted and spotted kinds are

The crowned lizard looks fierce, like most horned lizards, but is timid and gentle.

The Southern alligator lizard will bite, as do almost all related species, but the bite is not harmful or very painful.

mainly aquatic, and are seen generally when migrating from one pond or stream to another.

Most turtles live a very long time. Once my wife and I were visiting a woman in New York City, and we were invited to have a cup of coffee. As we went into the kitchen we had to step over a board about a foot high, which was fastened across the door opening. I thought it was a bit peculiar, but it wasn't any of my business, and I said nothing about it. We were sitting around the table talking, when suddenly I felt a nudge against my ankle, then an extremely sharp pain in my heel. I jumped out of my chair with an exclamation and discovered that I had a large snapping turtle fastened to my heel by its jaws. I grabbed it and yanked it off in surprise. The damn thing had nearly hamstrung me!

It developed that the turtle—which was named Herbert, by the way—was the woman's pet, and she had had it living on her kitchen floor for twenty-five years! The board was to contain the creature. The lady was very apologetic. It seems that in his quarter-century residence in the kitchen Herbert had never

Most turtles are harmless and have no defense except retreat into their shells. The snapper is an exception. It can strike almost like a snake and take off a finger. If you do pick one up by the tail, hold it out from your body or it can reach out and take a chunk out of your leg.

bitten anybody before. I offered a good recipe for turtle soup to our hostess, but I'm afraid it wasn't appreciated.

There are a great variety of lizards in the South—many more in these warmer states than there are in the North. In the South, too, there is much more superstition and fear of living animals than there is

The red-eared terrapin is the turtle sold by the tens of thousands as pets every year. Perhaps one in a thousand is cared for correctly and enjoys its existence.

among the Northerners. In saying this I do not mean to start a second Civil War, but it certainly is the truth, and I speak from personal experience as well as acquired knowledge.

I think it is possible that much of this fear and superstition was brought over from Africa with the hordes of slaves carried into the southern tier of the states, and a lot of it rubbed off on the white people living there. Tropical Africa harbors many poisonous species, and snakes, other reptiles, and insects can be a true hazard in an African village of mud or grass construction, so it is understandable that an African brought to this country would distrust any species he did not recognize and know to be harmless. While I may be in error here, it seems very logical, more so in view of the fact that many of the superstitions held in our South are also held by the tribal members of the African nations.

Not too long ago I was writing a book about reptiles, and, for the illustrations in that work, needed specimens of anything and everything I could get. My son

The wood turtle has a wonderfully sculptured carapace, colored with rich browns and yellows. It is an endangered species, protected by law.

Bill was stationed in the South, and I asked him to catch all the different kinds of lizards and reptiles he could and send them to me. He was a great help, but not until I had re-educated him. Every time he caught something, someone would start to scream about how deadly it was, or what it would do to him, or some other tomfool story, and he would let it go and write me, asking about it, describing the creature accurately so I would know what he was talking about.

One example was the five-lined skink. A skink is a kind of lizard, sleek, smooth, beautifully colored, and *absolutely harmless*. Down where Bill was this innocuous creature is called a scorpion, and it is held to be so deadly that even its breath can kill you! A scorpion itself is called a vinagaroon, and this is also a "deadly" creature. Wow! Those people must spend ninety percent of their time shaking in their boots at the uncountable hordes of venomous creatures waiting beyond their doors to do them in if they step outside.

Even the plastron of the wood turtle is beautifully marked with blotches of deep chestnut.

The comical little hognose snake, which I mention elsewhere, is in the South supposed to be so venomous and deadly that it can kill a person by hissing *at a distance of thirty feet!* The only safe way to kill this most dangerous of characters is with a rifle or shotgun, or, as one informant told me, to sneak up on one when it is asleep and chop off its head. Woe to you, though, if you wake it up and it opens its eyes and spots you. Then there is no possibility of escaping the wrath of this monster.

When I pointed out that snakes do not possess eyelids and therefore cannot close their eyes, his reply was a shrug of his shoulders and the inane statement,

The Southern painted turtle has a stripe down the middle of its carapace. All the painted turtles become quite tame.

"Well, them that I saw has." I marvel that he escaped with his life, since by his own admission he has looked into a hognose snake's eyes.

One most interesting species of reptile is the fence swift. It has rough scales and can run like a streak. Basking on a sunny branch or fence rail, it can spot you from a great distance, and it is nearly impossible to get close enough to catch them. Bill caught them with a very long pole and a silken noose; he became expert with this tool in the course of supplying me with specimens.

Our Southern anole is erroneously called a chameleon. It is not a chameleon, but it does have the ability to change the color of its skin from brown to green and back again. This change of color is not performed for the same purpose as that of the true chameleon from Africa and other parts of the Old World.

Anoles, like several other species of lizard, do not drink water out of pools, dishes, or puddles. They lap up drops of dew or rain hanging from the leaves

The Eastern painted turtle. Painted turtles are often seen crossing highways and roads.

among which they make their home. Unfortunately this trait is not known to many people who attempt to keep an anole—or to the pet-store proprietor selling it, for that matter—and, as a consequence, thousands upon thousands of the little animals perish miserably in captivity, when just this simple knowledge would keep them in good health. All you have to do is sprinkle water on some leaves in the anole's cage two or three times a day. A spray bulb such as is used for watering plants is ideal for the purpose.

If you have a greenhouse you might be interested in knowing that the common anole is a very valuable addition to the building. The heat and humidity make an excellent environment for the little lizards, and there is usually enough water in dew on the leaves and shelves to sustain the creature. In return for being

When you are cultivating your garden, you just might turn up a skink. They are harmless, and help control grubs and insects. The legs are virtually useless; within a few million years skinks will be legless.

The blue-bellied swift is an aptly named lizard.

permitted to live free in the greenhouse, the anole will keep your plants free from pests and parasitic insects. If you put several anoles in the greenhouse, there is an excellent chance that they will breed and rear young to keep up the population. You will be free from many of the harmful insects that often plague the hothouse owner. A few mealworms in a dish put in an accessible location will augment the diet of the helpers in case they have reduced the pest population so drastically that they have not enough to eat themselves. If you do not keep your greenhouse dripping, a spray of water on some of the heavier-leaved plants will furnish a liquid supply.

Are lizards dumb? Some of these creatures must operate on the very tiniest of ganglia instead of a brain. When we kept some Old World chameleons we fed them mealworms in an old glass ashtray. Around the edge of this container was a row of balls, molded into the glass as an ornamental border. The chameleons would stand patiently around the ashtray licking those little glass balls, thinking they were water, and trying to drink the drops. Finally we removed the tray and substituted a plain one.

The anole, often erroneously called a chameleon, can keep a greenhouse free of aphids and other harmful insects.

The true chameleons are a thing of wonder, though. Their feet are designed for twig living, and they act as tongs, gripping the smallest twig or tendril on vines with a mighty clasp. The eyes are independent of each other, and can swivel in all directions. It is not at all uncommon to have one looking up with one eye, and down or backward with the other. They perform a sort of syncopated waggle when sighting in on their prey, an unsuspecting insect that feels safe because it is several inches away from the animal. Then when the range is located to the chameleon's satisfaction, *zap!* The surprised insect is stuck on the sticky end of a tongue as long as the entire lizard, yanked off its perch into the cavernous mouth, and slowly and contentedly chewed and swallowed.

Chapter 6

Some Animal Stories

Throughout most of this book I have tried to discuss the wild animals you might see around your home in a systematic and orderly way, so that the book can serve as a handy reference. However, there is more to animals, and to people, and to their interaction, than can be expressed in such a general way. Therefore I would like to devote this long final chapter to some of the experiences my family and I have had. These are the experiences that account for my great interest in wild animals, and I hope you will have similar ones yourself.

Our property in the country is close to a ridge of mountains in the Catskill range. It is easy for animals to come down the unpopulated sides of the mountains and enter our acres. There are few houses between us and the ridge, and in the fall when food begins to become scarce, deer come off the mountain in great numbers. In the field in back of a friend's house about a quarter-mile from us, we counted fifty-eight deer one late afternoon.

For a couple of years the only building on my place was a very small cabin I had built in order to rear exotic moths for a book I was researching. The cabin was never intended to be lived in, but my wife and I began to use it as a place to sleep over when we came up each week to work the place. After the first year I added a wing to the cabin, to contain a kitchen and a bathroom. This wing had a door to the outside; the cabin had another door. With a kerosene space heater we were very snug in our little "country estate" and looked forward to spending our vacations there as well as our days off from our regular job.

This year we had been up for about a week of our vacation, busy with the moth rearing, and busy, also, clearing trees away for the proposed start of our house. We were sitting at the table basking in the warmth of the heater, for even though it was summertime, the evenings and nights were chilly.

We heard a scrabbling outside the cabin, and I looked out the window to see what it was, but it was already too dark to make anything out. Just then someone knocked at the back door. "Are you expecting anyone?" Gertrude asked me. I shook my head and went to open the door.

Outside stood a black bear. Knocking at the door for a handout, I suppose. We eyed each other for a moment. The bear said, "Funff!"

"Funff," I said back to him. He turned and departed in a curious, flat-footed loping gait, disappearing into the trees. I closed the door and went back to the table shakily. "Bear," I answered Gertrude's unspoken question.

"A *bear?* A big bear?"

I thought a moment. "About eleven feet high. Thirty feet or so long. Must have weighed three or four

101

tons. Got any coffee left?" After a cuppa I felt a little calmer, and the bear began to look more like a young bear, and not some monster that would be able to sweep our cabin off its foundations with a flick of one paw.

"Was there really a bear outside?"

"Yep. There really was. I guess we're living back to nature for real."

"What did he want?"

"Food, more than likely. He snorted at me. I snorted back at him. No bear is going to knock at my door and then snort at me when I open it."

"How big was he, really?"

"He looked about two and a half or three feet high, and maybe four or five feet long. Looked like a juvenile."

"Now I'll be afraid to go out at night."

"No problem. A bear isn't going to lie in wait for you and attack you when you open the door. If you see a bear around, just walk away from it and the chances are it will never molest you. Of course there are exceptions, but you do not have to live in fear of them. Anyway, I don't think they are all that plentiful around here."

A short time ago the conservation department called me to ask if I would be interested in an injured young fox. I drove down to the station to look at the animal. She was a beauty. Her coat glistened with good health, her eyes were bright, and her nose was wet and cold. The men at the station told me they simply hadn't the heart to shoot her. She had been hit on the road.

She was obviously lethargic from pain, and made no real attempt to bite or otherwise defend herself while I examined her. Her left hip was shattered in several places. In fact it was broken so badly that the entire area felt mushy under my prodding hands. I shook my head. When an animal was this badly injured there was little chance it would recover, and even if it did get over the broken bones, it probably would be unable to run down its fast prey in order to survive.

"Do you think you can do anything for her?" I was asked.

"I doubt it very much."

"Do you feel like trying? We just can't kill her, she's too pretty." The conservationist looked a bit sheepish. "Tell you what, suppose you take her and see if you can do anything for her. Then if you can't, *you* shoot her."

"In other words you want me to do your dirty work. Is that it?"

"Yeh. Something like that," he admitted.

I took the fox. I gathered her up in my arms, careful not to wrack her injury any more than I had to, and put her in a carrying cage and loaded it in my car. She whimpered but made no move to attack me. A closer examination when I had her home revealed an almost hopeless series of fractures.

Bandaging such a fracture is little short of impossible. The bandage can be put on all right, but the animal will leave it in place just long enough to get her teeth sunk into it to rip it off. I knew that there wasn't much chance of the hip healing unless it could be held in place for several weeks. Finally I hit upon the idea of immobilizing the animal, and selected a clay flue tile to do the job. These come in several sizes, all about two feet long, so I selected one into which the fox would just fit with difficulty. If you want a busy time one day, try to stuff a scared and injured fox

103

through a flue tile so small that the animal has to be pushed inside forcibly. I finally got her in, her head just sticking out of one end and her rump out the other, with the broken hip and that leg stuffed up in such a way that she could not wiggle it free.

The poor animal lived in the tile for several weeks. About every three days, I would slide her out far enough to let the circulation restore itself in her body, then put her back again, amid much protesting. In all that time she never tried to bite me. Throughout her entire confinement, I saw that she had food and water, and nothing more in the way of attention.

Each day I would go to the cage, plop down her food and water dishes, and walk away, paying her no attention. I particularly did not want to get her used to human attention, nor did I wish to tame her in any degree. Aside from the handling when she was examined, she was left entirely alone.

For food I used chicken parts, purchased in the supermarket. I also shot chipmunks and gave them to her whole. Every other day I gave her a ration of canned cat food into which I mixed an enormous dose of powdered penicillin.

After about four weeks I saw that she was squirming around within the tile, trying to free herself. I pulled her out of the tile and replaced that one with one large enough for her to crawl into when she wanted. Now began a period of observation. As long as I was in sight, she lay quietly in the tile. Whenever I disappeared from her vision, she would slowly ooze out of the tile and attempt to stand. The hip bones had knitted together, with thick calluses in several locations, which I could feel on examination. These would absorb later, I knew. At first the fox stood on three legs only, and walked with a three-legged gait. Later I

Just the tip of our injured fox's tail can be seen protruding from the flue tile which held her immobile while her leg healed.

noticed her gingerly putting her bad foot down. Finally she walked about her pen with a limp, but putting all her weight on all four feet.

After a week or so of this surreptitious movement I removed the tile from the pen. Now she could not hide from me any longer the fact that she could move about. Finally I would see her stand on both hind legs, as tall as possible, looking for a way out of the pen, and decided she was ready to return to the wild.

This presented a real problem to me. First of all, foxes—red foxes, at least—are monogamous, and I had no way of knowing where she came from. The conservation department was of no help either, because the animal had not been brought into the station by the person who had hit it. However, one thing was in the creature's favor. First, she was obviously a young female, probably whelped in the spring of the last year. This meant she would not have been mated. Next, she *was* a female, and it was early spring—the normal mating time for red foxes—so releasing her in strange territory should not be too dangerous for her. A male fox would be another story;

his chance of survival would be greatly lessened by liberating him in another fox's range. I simply had to take the chance that whatever fox was in command of the land surrounding my acres was not mated.

To help the creature on her way I did not just open the cage and shoo her out into the yard. Rather, the next morning after taking her food and water, I very "carelessly" left the latch open on the pen door. A few hours later I went out to look. The food dish was licked clean, the door was ajar, and the little wild creature was nowhere to be seen. She had taken advantage of my slipshod security and made her "escape" to the wild where she belonged.

I like to think of my little friend curled up in some snug den, nursing a litter of kits, with perhaps a fleeting memory once in a great while of the good rations she enjoyed during her convalescence, but I am afraid that is attributing a little too much to her mentality. However, for a long time after her escape I was careful to place food out at the border of the woods, and the food was always gone each morning. That's not to say that the fox got it—there are any number of wild creatures around my place, too many for me to be sure that one particular animal is feeding on my largess.

My first confrontation with a phoebe came about five years ago. At that time much of our present house had yet to be built, and we lived in one cabin, with a disconnected wellhouse, and a second building that served to house our garden tractor, tools, and the clothes washer and dryer. These three buildings were in line with one another, and now are all incorporated into the main house, but at that time we had to go outside the cabin to enter either the utility building or to take care of the well pump. I had an overhead garage door on the utility building, and a solid exterior door on the wellhouse. One spring evening I carelessly left the wellhouse door half open.

The next morning I discovered my mistake. When I started to close the door, I was assaulted by a dive-bombing bird of a species new to me at that time. Splatterings of mud on the door led my attention to the fact that this hysterical creature had begun building a nest of mud on top of the wellhouse door, preventing any chance of closing it. After considering the problem for a while, I decided that the nest had to go. I certainly could not risk the wellhouse being flooded in an unexpected downpour, because the well casing projected less than a foot up out of the ground, and it would not take much water to find its way down the hole to contaminate the well.

With apologies to the bird, who was hovering about in a dither, I scraped the gobby nest off the door and firmly closed it.

All that day, and for the next two days, I watched the bird make endless and fruitless attempts to stick a nest onto the outside of the door. She was determined to build her nest on that door, and nothing was going to stop her—except gravity. She simply could not make the mud stick to the door long enough to dry and support the structure.

Finally I took pity on her, and nailed a short board, shelflike, just over the door. She ignored the board for another day or so, still making a real mess of the door itself. Finally I took a handful of mud, slapped it on the board, and said to the little pest, "There! That's good, sticky mud. Build your nest out of that and stop this monkey business on the door." Strangely enough, she investigated the mud for some hours, and that evening I saw her begin to pick at it. Throughout the following day she was very active on the board, and soon I saw a new nest taking form.

She raised four babies that season. She was a phoebe.

By the next spring, I had altered the wellhouse, building on to it so that it now adjoined the utility building. Again I left a door open, this time the large overhead door to the washer and dryer. Sure enough, my little pesky friend came swooping into the building and proceeded to build her mud-and-moss nest on top of the fluorescent fixture. Unfortunately I did not notice the activity until it was too late. Since the weather was beautiful, I had been leaving the door open more or less constantly, and while I was partly aware of a flurry of wings as the mother bird stormed out of the building as I entered, I never thought of searching the place for a nest.

My first premonition of anything wrong was one day when I entered in search of a tool and saw a pile of droppings in the center of the floor. I stood looking at the mess when suddenly the phoebe dive-bombed me, yelling at the top of her lungs. A chorus of smaller shrieks joined in to call my attention to the light fixture, and, sure enough, four tiny heads were looking over the edge. At least they were the heads!

I confess to being somewhat of a softie. While my first impulse was to go get my shotgun and blow the feathers off the invaders, I couldn't bring myself to kill them. Nor could I toss out the nest, because it was obvious that the birds were not nearly fledged. I decided to leave them in residence until they left the nest, and this meant, naturally, that I had to leave the door open for mamma to fly in and out on her feeding missions.

The weather immediately broke, and the rain came down in torrents each day, practically flooding my machines and floating out my tools. Every time I would enter the place in search of a hammer or pliers, I would be met with such a demonstration of fury and pandemonium that finally I gave up in exasperation and stayed out of my own toolhouse, watching to see when the baby birds left the nest. About a week later the wonderful event arrived. Three of the birds sat in a row on the light fixture, and when I arrived at the door, took off in ungainly, uncertain flight, the mother bird accompanying them.

In a sudden overflow of frustration I snatched a short ladder, snapping it open as I carried it under the light. I mounted to the top, reached into the nest, grabbed the last chick, and flung it out the door. "Get *out* of here!" With a squawk of indignation the bird flapped to the nearest tree. The nest followed the bird out the door, and I attacked the pile of droppings with my shovel. No more of this.

By the third year I had added more to my house, and now the building which had been the utility building was incorporated in the main house. Gone was the overhead door, and in the center of that opening now a window looked out of one bathroom. Sure enough, the phoebe returned to make her new nest. She flew right into the windowpane, nearly breaking her neck. I almost wished she had, which is a strange thing for me. She then proceeded to splatter the window with mud in an attempt to make the nest stick. Finally she settled for the window sill. I did not. I scraped off the mud and washed the window. She began again, and again I ruined her work. Finally she got enough mud to stick under the roof overhang to harden into a nest base, and there she raised two sets of four babies each.

The fourth year, I had a reprieve. The phoebe rebuilt her last nest under the overhang and raised her two broods in peace.

By the fifth year I had added another room to the house, but had not completed closing the soffits before winter set in. In the spring my first job was to finish them. I worked around the room under the edge of the roof, nailing up the plywood soffit covers. On the last wall was the phoebe's nest!

I climbed the ladder to look at it. Inside were three phoebe eggs, plain white, about the size of jellybeans, and one large, speckled cowbird egg. I removed the nest and closed up the last soffit, rationalizing that the phoebe chicks were doomed anyway, because the cowbird chick on hatching would dump the smaller chicks out of the nest, and the mother phoebe would feed the invader as if it were her own.

This is the spring of the sixth year, and, as I write these words, I can hear the plaintive call outside: "Phoebe, phoebeee, phoebeee." I wonder where she will try this year. I am convinced that it will be in the one location that will cause me the most inconvenience. I have one assurance. At six, a phoebe is an old bird. She cannot last much longer. But then, I think of the number of chicks she has raised on my property, and wonder . . .

Before we moved to the country, we lived in an apartment in Westchester County, New York. It was a "garden-style" apartment house, composed of many two-story houses built on an erstwhile estate near the Hudson River. A brook ran through the grounds, in places in a very deep ravine—perhaps twenty-five feet lower than the banks.

On the road above, catchbasins had been built with rock-lined chutes leading from them down the bank ending at the brook. These supplied a path for rainwater to run off the street, and at times during a hard downpour, the brook became a raging torrent.

Over the years the rock chutes had become covered with wet moss, and, especially after a rainstorm, were as slippery as ice.

One night just as I was getting ready to go to bed a scream came through the night, loud and clear. At first I thought someone had whacked his child for some reason or other. Then again the screaming began, and now it sounded like a dog or other animal had been hit on the road but not killed. It was raining lightly, so I put on a jacket and went out into the grounds with my flashlight to see what was going on.

A light or two came on in other apartments as I made my way along the driveway toward the road. A bridge crossed the brook at the exit gate from the estate, and when I drew near the bridge I heard the cries coming from the brook. Scrambling and slipping down the bank, I shone my light at the water. At the bottom of one of the chutes, waist-deep in the fast-running brook, stood a very young raccoon, his head thrown back, yelling at the top of his lungs for his mommy. He was drenched to the skin, and from the bits of moss and smears of algae on his coat it was plain to see what had happened.

Trotting along the road above, he had either entered the catchbasin to get out of the rain, or what was more likely, stuck his inquisitive nose inside to see what was in there. He stepped on the wet moss and suddenly shot down the chute and landed with a mighty splash in the cold rushing water below. Probably the wits were scared out of him in the process, and

111

he wasn't at all shy about telling the world of his distress. You can imagine the racket he made at one o'clock in the morning.

I squatted down and shone my light on him. "What's all this racket about?" The sorry little beast took one look at me, then reached out with both hands and grabbed me around the neck, hauling himself out of the water to my shoulder, and holding on for dear life. I wore him back to the apartment, the water running out of his fur down my neck.

"Was it a dog?" my wife asked from the warm bed. I stopped to pick up a large bath towel before entering the bedroom.

"No. It was the newest member of our family." I tossed her the towel and bent over. "Peel him off me, will you?" The little fellow hung on for several minutes, refusing to give up his security. Finally, by pulling one hand off at a time, Gertrude was able to dislodge him and wrap him in the towel. While we dried him off he churred softly in contentment.

I had nothing in the house to feed a raccoon, so I offered a saucer of warmed milk. He immediately buried his nose in the dish and lapped as though milk was going out of style, all the time trying to breathe with his nostrils under milk. The result was a froth of bubbles all over his face. That named him, and Bubbles he was from then on.

He stayed the night in the bathroom with the door closed. At least a tiled floor would not be hard to clean. An hour or two after we went to sleep we awakened to a mighty crash. We rushed into the bathroom and were met with a litter of glass and assorted pills on the floor, and another litter in the washbasin, but no Bubbles. Then his nose poked around the sliding door of the medicine cabinet. Bubbles had slid open one door, swept the shelf free of obstructing bottles and jars, and then climbed up into his snug den for the balance of the night!

An apartment is no place for a raccoon. As far as that is concerned, I do not believe that an apartment is the place for any species of animal pet, except, perhaps, for a sedentary cat or a cage bird, or an aquarium of exotic fishes. Animals just do not belong in a confining environment. I know there are many people who will disagree with me on this, but that does not alter the fact that dogs, raccoons, any animal in fact, should be permitted to roam at will in the outdoors. This does not imply that you should keep a dog free outside, to run all over the neighborhood, inflicting its unwanted and unwelcome presence on your neighbors, either. If you want to keep such a pet, then you should be prepared to erect or have erected a sizable and substantial pen with a run for the animal. It can be let out of this place accompanied by some person who will keep it in check. Keeping dogs is much like smoking. You might like it, but it makes the people around you suffer, and nonsmokers as well as non-dog-lovers have rights, too.

The next morning I took Bubbles and drove about a mile down the road to a wooded area. Here I found a nice tree with a convenient fork about ten feet up. With some difficulty I managed to get Bubbles to sit in the fork. As soon as I started back to the car, he started tuning up. It is literally amazing to hear the amount of noise one small 'coon can produce. Hardening my heart, I drove back home.

"He'll be all right," I rationalized to Gertrude over lunch. "He'll holler for a while, then climb down and go hunt up his mommy."

"Just the same, I think you ought to make sure,"

she replied. We finished our lunch, then drove down the road. Bubbles was still sitting in the crotch of the tree, his arms around one of the trunks. The moment we drove up he began to yell. With a sigh I turned the car around and we went back home.

Just before supper Gertrude began looking sorrowfully at me, and kept it up until finally I gave in. Once more we drove to the tree. Bubbles was still there, and screeched when we drove up. I climbed up and let him come back on my shoulder.

That night we fed him on a can of sardines and some bread soaked in milk. He was famished. He was with us for a week. Some week! If I stopped walking he would bump into my heels. He walked with me everywhere I went, but simply would not walk beside me. Instead he crammed in between my feet so I had to waddle along trying to push him to one side or the other.

I walked him several times a day. Exploring everything about him, it never occurred to Bubbles to do his business and get it over with. Instead, he would wait until he was back inside, then immediately find the most inconvenient spot to relieve himself. All that exercise had activated his apparatus something fierce! It is practically impossible to housebreak a wild animal, and Bubbles was no exception.

Finally I found a woman who had a nice little female raccoon. Yes, she would love to have a male. Bubbles finally left us for what I hope were happier surroundings. Gertrude shed a small tear. "You couldn't help liking the little mutt," she said in justification.

"Daddy, can I keep a pet?" Bill was about twelve or thirteen at the time.

"What kind of pet?"

"A 'possum."

"I really don't think a 'possum would make such a good pet, Bill. Anyway, I wouldn't know where to find one without going all through the woods looking for them. Also, 'possums usually stay a little farther south than here."

He pulled a roll of paper from his pocket. "I've already got one," he said, unwrapping a tiny squirming pink naked creature. Eyes tightly shut, it looked as though it had just been born.

"Where did you find that?"

"In the park. A man told me it was a 'possum. Can I keep it, Daddy?"

"First of all, I don't think it is a 'possum. The head is too round, and its nose is too blunt. Also the tail doesn't look like a 'possum's tail should. Besides that, if it is a 'possum, feeding it will be a problem. Feeding any animal this small will be a problem, for that matter. Maybe you'd better put it back where you found it."

Bill looked at me sadly. "You know, Dad," he said seriously, "If I do put it back, it'll only die. The mother 'possum won't take it back. The man told me so."

"I don't think that man knew much about what he said," I told my son. "First of all, baby 'possums live in their mother's pouch. That's number one. Then, if one fell out of the pouch, it would crawl right back in. That's number two. Number three is, what are you going to feed it?" I poked the thing in my hand. It wiggled a bit, opening its mouth. It certainly didn't look like a marsupial to me. "It looks more like a rodent," I told Bill.

"What kind?"

"Maybe a squirrel. Maybe just a rat." The tiniest of

squeaks came from my handful. "Whatever it is, we'd better get it a lot warmer, and get something into its tummy."

While Bill held the little creature in his cupped hands, I got out the electric heating pad and fitted it into a carton. With a couple of old bath towels on top of the pad, and the control set at low, I thought it would make a snug enough nest. A cover placed on the carton leaving a small strip open would further contain the heat and keep the baby from becoming chilled.

We warmed a little milk, added a spoonful of honey, and stirred in a little water to dilute the mixture. An eyedropper served as a nipple. The animal took to it as though it was feeding from its mother. We could see the formula run down its throat and slowly fill its stomach, right through the pink transparent skin. Very convenient. We merely fed it until it filled up.

It survived, but didn't seem to grow very much in a week. I was under the impression that a week meant a considerable increase in size and weight in all creatures like this. I telephoned the Bronx Zoo and asked to speak to the curator of small mammals. "What would you feed a baby squirrel?" I asked.

"How old is it?"

"I don't know. Very young—its eyes are still closed."

"Forget it," was the disheartening reply. "You don't stand much chance of keeping a squirrel that young alive. I'd say just flush it down the john and put it out of its misery."

"I really don't think it is all that miserable." I hung up. We got a bottle of liquid baby vitamins, Pablum, strained baby fruits and vegetables, and evaporated milk. With these we concocted a formula that was designed to have a supply of proteins, carbohydrates, fat, and minerals as well as supplementary vitamins. Pogo took whatever we filled her up with, and with no complaints.

Since she was supposed to have been a 'possum, her name just naturally became Pogo. She didn't grow rapidly. As a matter of fact, I suppose in the outside wild she would have been called a runt. As time passed, we became certain that it was not a 'possum, and more sure she was a squirrel, even if her fur was not covering her nor colored gray.

Thirty-six days after Bill brought her home she opened her eyes. That told us she was only one day old when he found her, because a gray squirrel opens its eyes in thirty-seven days. Now she really took an interest in everything around her, and, it seemed to us, her growth perked up considerably. Soon she was covered with soft gray fur, and her little tail had short fuzz all along its length. At about five weeks she began to try to nibble at things, and we decided it was time for us to wean her.

First we shoved soft fruits in her mouth. She got some down, but it was obviously difficult, especially banana. She choked on that. So we rammed the stuff down her throat with a Q-tip. The padding on the end protected her mouth. We ground up nuts and mixed them with baby fruits, and poked her full of this mess. A friend who happened in at feeding time one day remarked, "She's a real muzzleloader, isn't she?"

Each day we gave her a shelled walnut, and in a couple of days saw little nibble marks on one, so we added several kinds of nuts to her diet. Celery, cherries, apple, almost any fruit—she was especially fond of seedless grapes—carrots, green beans, and fresh peas. She ate them all. She went out of her mind with

delight the first time we offered her a piece of canta-
loupe. She ate it until there was nothing but a paper-
thin peel left, then begged for more.

In the meantime we had been giving some thought
to how to house her when she finally left her carton. I
finally made a large cage out of hardware cloth, and
this we stood in a corner of the dining room in front of
a window. The cage was large enough to let Pogo sit in
the top branches of a small tree fastened inside and
look out the window. She spent most of her time in the
tree, but I noticed she had great difficulty getting up
it.

It finally dawned on us that she didn't know how to
climb. This thought had never occurred to us, but after
it did, we realized that everything must be taught to
baby things, including climbing, I suppose, to baby
squirrels.

I took her outside and stuck her on the trunk of a
roughly barked tree. Moving her legs, I said, "This is
the way little squirrels climb." Marching her up and
down for a day or so was all that was needed. Soon she
would walk off my hand and climb up the trunk by
herself. However, she wasn't all that surefooted,
because once when she encountered a small branch,
she lost her hold while trying to get around it and fell
to the ground, landing squarely on her nose. She sat
on my shoulder crying until the bleeding stopped,
then we tried again. She discovered that climbing
down was a lot different than climbing *up,* and I had
to show her the flattened hind-leg-waddle that they
use in this maneuver.

For this lesson I took her to a very tall tree outside
the dining-room window. She scampered up the trunk
until she was nearly forty feet up, and there she clung,
looking down at me, and not knowing how to turn

118

around to descend. I called for an hour, but she hung on for dear life. The longest ladder I could find was too short by several feet, but I went up it to the top. Pogo only moved a little higher as I neared her perch.

For two days Pogo sat in that tree. Fortunately the nights were warm by then. The afternoon of the second day I stood beneath the tree calling her. Suddenly three feet gave way, and she fell from the trunk, one hind foot still stuck to the bark. This served to turn her nose down, and she grabbed hold of the bark and ran down to the ground, over to me, and up my leg to my head.

She learned, in the weeks following, to go up and down with equal ease, and so I made a runway of hardware cloth reaching from her cage over the sill and out the window. I cut a board to fit under the window to close the remaining space. Pogo could now run free whenever she wished, or remain in her cage. She had a ball!

As the summer progressed she ranged more and more in the yard, finally remaining outdoors all day, but coming in to feed and sleep, at dusk. Once she did not come home, and we waited for two days. When she finally did arrive, she was a sorry-looking creature. One ear was torn; there were several patches of fur missing, and half the hair was pulled out of her tail. Obviously she had had a fight and come off second best. I remembered the territorial belligerence of animals, and realized that, by letting her run free, we were placing her in the territory of other squirrels. I had hoped that having the cage to run to, she wouldn't get into trouble, but evidently that wasn't the case. We still let her run, however, and hoped she would learn.

One day she brought home another squirrel. He was

enormous, with a beautiful coat and a tail like a plume. He came as far as the house, and sat while Pogo entered her runway. She sat in the opening and called to him, but he would not respond. Day after day he came with her, and I offered him nuts. When one day he climbed on the window sill to take them I knew half the battle of making friends was over. After a few more days he sat while I offered him a nut from my fingers. Not quite yet. He jumped down, but didn't leave. He readily took the nut after I placed it on the sill.

It was nearly a week before he gingerly reached out and snatched a nut from my fingers, immediately running across the yard to sit and eat it. Another week and he would sit on the sill to open the treat, eyeing me warily as he fed on the succulent kernel. I usually gave him a walnut in the shell. Sometimes a hazelnut. Once I handed him an almond. He took it, examined it, turned it around and around in his hands, smelled it, and then handed it back to me. "You don't like almonds?" I asked in surprise. Surprise, not that he didn't like almonds, but that he handed it back.

The next day I again tried an almond, and again he handed it back. Thus began a game. Whenever he came to the sill I would hand him the almond, watching his careful examination. When he handed it back I would offer him a walnut or another nut. He would take it, reach out and very gently nibble the knuckle on my outstretched finger, then sit up and start to gnaw through the shell. Friends used to come and watch the performance of returning the almond with amazement.

Pogo lived with us for two years. The second summer she stayed out several nights in a row at several different times. Toward fall Bill found her on the road. She had been hit by a car. The entire family mourned her death.

Once during our sojourn in the South, the professor of science at the local university called me.

"Want a baby armadillo?"

I did. I had never seen a living specimen, and thought it would be fun.

"Better bring something to take it home in."

"What do you have it in now?"

"One of our rat cages." That was easy; I had a couple of small cages that I used for hamsters, so I put one of them in the car and drove to the school. When I arrived at the room my friend was at his desk. The classes were over. He jerked his head over his shoulder, and I followed the motion. I had forgotten that in a university, a rat cage was a massive affair that could contain about fifty animals. In the corner was a heavy-meshed box containing the baby armadillo. This "baby" was about eighteen inches long, and ten high. It was sitting quietly. I reached inside and put my hand on the animal's back. It stood up, pinning my hand against the top of the cage. Since standing the creature was as high as the inside of the cage, it followed that my hand had to go somewhere. It did. It waffled through the inch-square steel mesh! The thing beneath my hand was absolutely immovable. I squatted for a while, waiting for the bones in my hand to give way. "Goose her," said the professor, over his shoulder.

I rammed my other hand under her rear end and she shot all four legs sideways, falling flat on the floor. I yanked my hand out of the cage and looked at the wonderful pattern of valleys forever pressed into the back.

"Did you bring a cage?"

"Well, not exactly. That is, the one I brought isn't big enough. I thought you said a *baby* armadillo."

"That's a baby. Born this spring." He walked over and looked at my hand. "Hurt?"

"Well, it has felt better." I looked at him. "You know, I think you knew what was going to happen. Didn't you? *Didn't you?*"

He started to laugh. "Had a good idea you didn't know too much about these animals."

"Well, suppose you bring me up to date."

"They won't bite, but watch out for their claws. Main diet is insects, but I suppose they'd eat anything they can get into their mouth. Four young of identical sex each time. This one's a female. Cute little critter, isn't she?" I saw nothing cute about that army tank at the moment.

Close up, an armadillo is the most improbable thing on earth. The shell over the body is broken into nine bands at the middle, permitting it to curl up into a ball as protection from its enemies. The belly is soft and covered with warts and long straggly hairs. The head is long and pointed, with a tiny piglike snout and tiny eyes under large flapping ears. The feet have enormous claws, hard and sharp, and I could see that it was good advice the teacher had given me. "You can take it in that cage, and return it when you are through."

At home I dumped the animal out of the cage in the back yard. She immediately took off for the tall timber, but I smacked a hand down on her back, pinning her to the ground. Gingerly I worked both hands around her middle until I could pick her up without being clawed to the bone.

We had a pair of toy chihuahuas at that time, and

The armadillo is a strange creature, and in my experience, not a satisfactory house pet.

Gertrude had just put out their lunch—a plateful of hot scrambled eggs. They were evidently too hot for the dogs, who were waiting for them to cool when I entered the door with Alice in my hands. Since it was so improbable, the name Alice from Wonderland came to my mind as a natural name for the beast. I stood holding it so Gertrude could look it over.

She stared at Alice in amazement. "I don't believe it!" she exclaimed. At that moment Alice gave a great heave and thumped to the floor like a bowling ball. Nothing daunted, she rolled over on her legs and scuttled over to the hot eggs.

Like a vacuum cleaner, her long slender snout went back and forth across the plate, leaving it completely empty and polished clean. Then, after a piggy look around the room and a grunt of satisfaction, she scurried behind the range. It took an hour to dislodge her and get her into a large, heavy cage in the yard.

123

It took her about five minutes to rip the side out of the cage and waddle out. I caught her and took her into the house, shutting her up in the bathroom until I could make a suitable enclosure out of very heavy hog wire. It wasn't finished by evening, so we decided to let Alice stay in the bathroom overnight.

She scrabbled at the door without letup, and finally I went in and put her in the bathtub. That ought to quiet her, I thought to myself. At least, she couldn't get out of the tub. At suppertime we heard an occasional loud thump. On investigation we found Alice climbing out of the tub over the faucets, then climbing right up the slick tile wall by the simple expedient of locking her steel-hard claws in the grouting between. That wall was a broad highway for an armadillo. Reaching the ceiling, she would attempt to walk out on that, slipping, naturally, and sliding down the wall to land in the tub with a thump. Enough of that. I could just picture us trying to sleep with that going on.

I took her out to my little shop and shut her up there. I figured she should not be able to hurt any tools, and I pulled out the plugs of the machines so she couldn't flip the switches. In the morning no Alice was in sight. In the smooth sheetrock walls were several large holes, clawed in, then licked or chewed out. Plaster was on everything. She hadn't missed investigating a single tool or machine. Nearly every hand tool was on the floor.

As I stood inside looking around at the mess I was afforded a barrage of small round fecal pellets from Alice, who was comfortably lying on one of the ceiling rafters. (The ceiling had not yet been put in.)

I got the cage, held it under her, and knocked her off her perch. I slammed the door shut, loaded it up, and drove back to the university, stopping at a wooded place on the way. Opening the cage, I unceremoniously dumped Alice out on the ground, seized her by the middle, turned her to point to the hinterland, and gave her a whack on the behind. "Get out of here and don't come back!"

At the school the professor accepted the cage with a smile. "How's she doing?"

"Just fine," I replied with a straight face. "I guess she's pretty contented by now. She's had a lot of exercise and good food under her belt since yesterday." I wasn't about to disclose any details of her short sojourn with the Villiards.

Deliver me from armadillos.

Many times a wild animal may be handled without consequence. Our apartment house had a large recreation room in the basement of one of the buildings. The windows to the room were high up on the walls, since the room itself was mainly below ground level. In the summer, these windows were often left open by the tenants using the room, and I used to check them each morning.

One day as I entered the recreation room I smelled a faint musk odor. Skunk. I looked all around the room, but couldn't see anything. There were several cabinets, chairs, tables and other equipment all around the room, and if there was a skunk in the room, it had managed to find a spot to hide in that was beyond me. "O.K., fellow," I said to the seemingly empty room, "I'll be back when it gets dark, and then you watch out."

That night I got half an apple and headed for the rec room, accompanied by Gertrude. We met a girl on the walk and in reply to her query told her we were going to look for a skunk. When we got into the room I turned on the lights. Sure enough, the skunk was right in front of the door. It was a juvenile. I squatted down and held out the apple, talking softly to it.

Several children came to the window and watched, obviously rounded up by the girl we had met. They made so much racket that I had to tell them to quiet down until I caught the skunk. Keeping up my steady talk, I walked over to the little creature, which cowered in a corner as I approached. I reached out and held the apple right under its nose. It was evidently hungry, because I could see its nose quiver as it smelled the apple. I lifted up my hand to touch its nose and it gingerly took a nibble. As soon as it had the apple in its mouth, I reached out and began to scratch it under the front arm. That was just too good to resist, and the little skunk munched contentedly on the apple while I scratched under first one arm, then the other. As soon as it finished the fruit I slid my hand under its tummy and lifted it off the floor, immediately placing my other hand under all four feet for security. One thing that will engender great fear in animals is the lack of adequate support. This is the reason why they squirm so frantically in an attempt to escape when people pick them up by the body, letting their legs dangle in the air without anything under them.

The skunk snuggled down in my hands and I went over and opened the door. As I stepped outside the gang of kids scattered like a covey of quail flushed by a hound. I carried the animal down by the brook and released it, and it ambled off with great dignity.

The word soon got around. Among the kids I was some kind of nut. "Mr. Villiard picks up skunks!"

One of the troubles with living in an apartment is that if you do like animals, and do want to keep some, you really are limited to a cat or an aquarium or a cage with a bird inside, as I've pointed out before. That is, you *should* be limited to something like that. It is no fun for either the animal or yourself to coop up creatures that are not sedentary in a small apartment. Or in a large apartment, for that matter. Yet, there are many people who do just that, calling themselves animal lovers. They are really only satisfying their own desires, because if they gave any serious thought to the matter they would conclude that the animal would be far better off in the outdoors.

In suburban living, this is not so much of a problem, since the pet or captive creature can be kept outdoors in a more or less roomy cage or pen, and is not so confined. Also, the cleanup process is greatly simplified.

For a time, while I was attempting to become a writer, I worked as an apartment-house superintendent. This work gave me a place to live, utilities, and a moderate salary, but most of all, it gave me a great deal of personal time that I could devote to writing, since when I rolled out of bed in the morning I was already at work, and after my day was done I was already at home, eliminating any travel time each day. Those hours were most useful to me.

However, it was a bit hard on the kids. They wanted pets, and I had to put my foot down. I don't happen to like cats, and I wouldn't have one around. I refused them a dog because dogs were not permitted in the house, and I was totally in agreement with this restriction. The older boy had his aquarium and raised fancy guppies. While we had Pogo, the little squirrel, everyone was happy, but her stay with us was not long.

Bill was then about fourteen years old. One afternoon when he had come home from school he came to my desk and stood there silently. From experience I knew he wanted something. I looked a question at him. He had one hand in his jacket pocket. "Daddy, can I keep a snake?"

"What kind?"

"I don't know." He took his hand out of his pocket, clutching a balled-up snake about two feet long. I looked at it. A northern watersnake. Notorious for their nasty dispositions, and for the fact that they seldom become really tame. They bite on little provocation, and I knew that they feed poorly in captivity.

"Did he bite you?" I saw a few spots of blood on Bill's arm.

"Just a little when I first caught him. Can I keep him, Daddy?"

"Go put some iodine and a Band-aid on the bite, and then I think you had better take it back where you found it and let it go."

"Why?" His eyes were ready to fill up.

"Mainly because these watersnakes do not make good pets. They won't feed in captivity, and they just wither away and finally starve to death. They bite all the time, and are generally nasty creatures. Is that reason enough?"

"Couldn't I just try it for a little while? If he doesn't eat or if he bites me all the time I'll let him go."

"All right. Try it for a couple of days." I couldn't deny him the effort.

That darn snake promptly made a liar out of me. It was so tame that Bill could tie it in knots. Three turns around his wrist made a living bracelet, which he wore as he rode his bike around the neighborhood. The snake never even made an attempt to leave his arm as long as Bill wore him. After that initial bite, it never again opened its mouth except to eat whatever Bill offered it in the way of food—small fish, netted from a nearby pond; an occasional frog, salamander, or tadpole; sardines, of all things, still greasy with their oil; an assortment of foods most improbable for a snake—all were taken with equal gusto.

Bill wore it to school. He became the envy of all the boys he knew, and finally one day at school he was persuaded to take it off his arm to let a friend play with it. The snake promptly slithered away from the friend, and went down the drain of the lab sink where they had been playing with it.

Bill was heartbroken. He haunted the lab until he was turned out by the school superintendent. Finally, after two days, he posted a notice on the bulletin board in the school hall, offering a fifty-cent reward to any-one returning his pet. His week's allowance. The day after that, the superintendent caught him as he was leaving for home. Dangling from his hand was Bill's little reptilian friend. It had finally come back up out of the drain.

By the time winter had arrived, Bill's enthusiasm for the snake had begun to wane. He fed it only sporadically. Finally I could stand it no longer, and I bought two goldfish to feed it. After that it was a pair of goldfish every other day to keep the boy's snake going. I told Bill several times that he was going to have to do something about his snake, because I did not want to take the responsibility of caring for it.

Actually the responsibility was not that onerous. It was the principle of the thing. It was Bill's pet, not mine, and I did not want him to shirk his duties. If he was going to keep a pet, he was going to have to take care of it. Not that I didn't realize that he was behaving just as a normal fourteen-year-old would.

Gertrude and I kept the snake in goldfish through the winter. In the spring, after the thaw and when the weather warmed up, I delivered my ultimatum. "Take it back where you found it and release it."

Bill cried and pleaded. I was adamant. "Nope. You had your chance and muffed it. You let your mother and me take care of it all winter, which leads me to believe you aren't interested any more. Out it goes."

With wet eyes Bill wrapped the snake around his wrist for the last time and rode off on his bike. He returned about an hour later, subdued and unhappy.

"Did you let it go?" I asked him.

"Yes."

The next day he was back to normal, and within the week he seemed to have entirely forgotten the reptile. I'll always wonder how that critter made such a monkey out of me.

The science teacher in the local school is much interested in birds. Raptorian birds, for the most part—birds of prey such as owls, hawks, eagles, and similar species. Each year he puts out nesting boxes for them, and each year he traps many different kinds, banding them and training some of them in falconry. Often he takes very young chicks from the nest boxes in order to rear them to the hand. All this is by way of readying himself to become a specializing ornithologist rather than continuing as a general science teacher.

A few years ago he was muttering unhappily because in one box he had put out for kestrels, a family of flying squirrels had taken abode. My ears perked up at the news. I had never even seen a flying

One of our flying squirrels gets a treat. We kept a family of these beautiful animals for five years.

squirrel. These animals are one of our most common species, yet very few persons have ever seen them. The reason is that flying squirrels are completely nocturnal, and even when they are out in the open, they are silent little creatures.

They do not actually fly. They glide on extended flaps of skin held out rigidly between their front and rear legs. This forms a kind of kite or parachute. Their tails are densely furred, and the fur grows out from each side of the tail, making a flat blade that the animal uses to guide his flight. By tipping the tail up or down he can regulate his climb or ascent, much as the ailerons of an airplane. Their power of flight is astonishing. From the top of a tall tree, they can jump out into the air and glide over 150 feet in a graceful arc.

I was most anxious to see some of these elusive neighbors, and asked my friend Bill if he could figure out a way to catch them. He said he knew how, so we set out together to gather them in. First we made a tube of window screening, about four inches in diameter and perhaps a foot long. Taking his ladder on his

131

jeep, Bill and I went to the location of the kestrel box, where together we put the ladder up so he could reach the nest. He held the screen tube over the hole in the box, near the open end, then, reaching out with a small rock, he banged on the nest box sharply. The little squirrel jumped out of the opening without looking where she was going, and Bill immediately squashed shut the open end of the tube. We had her! Neat. He dropped the screen to me, with the squirrel inside. A very surprised little animal. Then he reached into the nest box. "There are some babies in here," he called down to me.

"If we take the mother, we'd better take the babies too." He scrabbled around in the nest of dry leaves.

"Feels like two, nearly full grown." He hauled them out and stuffed them into his pocket to climb down the ladder.

At home I fixed up a nice cage for the little animals, with a box for a nest, and with plenty of material for her to fashion another nest out of. I put the whole thing on a shelf in the boiler room where it was nice and warm. Both the mother and the babies were crawling with fleas.

I purchased a ninety-day flea collar for cats, made a tube of hardware cloth so the rodents couldn't gnaw the collar, and wrapped it up in that, bending the whole thing into a large circle. This I placed inside the nest box so that when the animals were in the nest they had to sit inside the collar. Within three days there wasn't a single flea on any of the three animals. I left the collar inside, however, in order to get any fleas that hatched from eggs already laid.

The little creatures adapted to captivity with no problem. The mother even let me touch her after the first day. I fed them on nuts and fruit, with a little milk and honey in a dish outside the nest box. After about a week the two babies were seen outside the box in the evening. In another couple of days I noticed them sleeping curled up in a corner of the cage. I poked them through the entrance, back into their nest. A couple of hours later they were again outside the box. Again I stuck them back, only to find them in the same corner the next time I looked. I opened the nest box to see what the reason for the eviction was. Mommy squirrel was curled up in a half-circle nursing five of the tiniest babies imaginable!

I built a cage in the yard, four feet square and eight feet high, and put a small tree inside, and also a section of hollow log with a top and bottom fastened to it for a nesting box. I moved my family out there. Now that they were free of fleas they were the sleekest little creatures I had ever seen. They were so soft that it was difficult to hold them in the hand; they'd just ooze out of your grip. They have very sweet faces, with a Disney-like expression, and never a bit of aggressiveness in their behavior. They lived with us for five years, and were the most endearing little pets we have ever had.

Opossums are strange creatures. They are the only marsupials indigenous to this country. They are also very primitive animals. Because of the unfortunate expression of an opossum's mouth, it looks ferocious and wicked. It really isn't at all that way, but rather very timid. The opossum has fifty teeth in its mouth, and the lips are curled back as though in a snarl, exposing many of the fifty businesslike fangs. The impression is that the animal is just getting ready to tear you limb from limb.

Another strange thing about opossums is their

method of feeding the young. Inside the marsupial pouch are thirteen teats. The mother opossum gives birth to as many as twenty young at a time. The babies are not much larger than a bumblebee, and as soon as they are born, they crawl into the pouch, seek out a teat and fasten their mouth to it. That is, the lucky first thirteen babies do. The remainder wander about until they starve to death!

Once fastened to the teat, the baby animal does not let go, but remains hanging onto it, suckling as it needs food. They nurse in this fashion for eight weeks, at which time they are weaned and take their regular food.

Shortly after I became known as a writer in the area of natural history, people began calling me for information about all kinds of animals. One such call was from the state conservation department, asking if I would be willing to foster a couple of baby opossums. I said I would, and they said one of their men was going to be near my place that evening and would drop them off to me.

When the man arrived, the "couple" of baby opossums turned out to be twelve—almost an entire litter. The female had been killed by a car, and the babies

Seven of our dozen baby opossums cluster around their dish.

One of our opossums, nearly full-grown—big enough to care for itself, and too big, along with its eleven siblings, to share our board any longer.

had finally left the pouch when the supply of milk was cut off. I didn't know how to turn away ten of the helpless creatures, so took in the dozen. Of course the care and feeding immediately fell to my wife, with what help I could give her.

The first thing we had to do was figure out a formula which would supply sufficient nutrients to the babies. I used Similac with iron, a prepared baby formula sold in cans in grocery and drug stores. To this we added a few drops of ABDEC baby vitamins, a little honey, and a little powdered Pablum—another babyfood cereal—to thicken the fluid a little, and to add some needed ingredients.

We discovered that it was nearly impossible to feed the creatures out of an eyedropper, because they simply never keep still long enough to get the end of the dropper into their mouths. They wiggle and squirm without letup, and finally we gave it up as a bad job.

Next we tried letting them feed from a shallow dish, but they didn't know enough to lap up the food. Don't ever make the mistake of giving an opossum credit for having a brain cell in working order. They are about as stupid an animal as I can think of.

After an interminable length of time working with them, we hit on the idea of dipping a fingertip into the food and ramming that against the nose. The baby would lick the formula off the finger. Gradually we brought their snouts down to the level of the plate and then rammed their noses into the food. They would rear back and lick their noses clean. We would dip them in once again, and repeated this procedure until finally, after we had decided they would just have to starve to death, they began timidly to lick at the edge of the liquid in the dish. From then on they learned to lap up their supper with gusto. The formula agreed with them, and they grew apace.

It was also impossible, however, to keep them from wading around in their food dish every time they fed, which was several times each day. To help keep the mess they made confined to a reasonable area, we spread several thicknesses of newspaper on the table, put the dish in the middle and the little babies around the dish, and let them have at it. Then we rolled up the papers and disposed of them.

Soon we had twelve fat little babies. Then we had twelve fat big babies. Then we had twelve hungry opossums about the size of kittens, not nearly able to fit inside the carton which was their temporary home. When they got to be about as big as a cat, we called up the conservation department. Would they like to have twelve well-fed and frisky juvenile opossums back? Not on your life, said they.

Gertrude and I discussed the opossum population density of our few acres, and decided that it was becoming a simple matter of survival—for us. We liberated the tribe on our backwoods land. What a shock that must have been to the 'possum-in-residence!

Ordinarily one does not think of a robin as an aggressive bird, but as a kind of jolly, alert, colorful creature solely interested in pulling the fattest and longest worms up through the roots of your lawn grass.

One day late in April my youngest son and I were sitting on the cabin porch. We had not yet begun to build the house, and the dwelling consisted of a ten-by-seventeen-foot cabin with a full-length porch added to the west side. It was raining a veritable downpour, windless, the water pounding straight down to the soaked ground. About twenty feet away was a pine tree; its lower branches sagged with the weight of the water on the needles. It was about nine o'clock in the morning, and we sat disconsolately on the porch wondering how we were going to be able to do the day's work. I had about decided that the day was going to be wasted as far as construction work was concerned, when a shrill shriek sounded from the pine tree, and a robin flew out of the branches to dive at one of the lower limbs in a frenzy.

Bill looked at me and asked, "I wonder what that was all about?" Meanwhile the robin dived again and again at the branch. Finally we both got up and slipped into our ponchos. As we approached the tree both of us spotted the trouble at the same time. Stretched along one of the bottom branches was an enormous black rat snake. It was nearly six feet long, large for the species, and it was balanced exquisitely along the branch with alternate loops of its body hanging down both sides of the limb. Further examination of the tree revealed a nest higher up, in which were several chicks, the heads peering up over the rim of the nest. The male robin sat next to the nest while the female was diving at the snake.

Our presence there did not seem to deter the frantic bird from the protection of her nest and babies. She would fly high above the tree, then dive at the snake, pulling up short just as she was about to hit it, and deliver a vicious peck at the unprotected back of the reptile. Already there were several spots along the length of the creature where the skin had been punctured and blood puddles formed, slowly washing away in the torrential rain. Bill started looking around the ground.

"What are you after?"

"A stick."

"Leave them alone," I cautioned. "We shouldn't interfere. This is a part of nature that should work itself out without our influencing it one way or the other."

"What about the baby birds?"

"Are you concerned because they are baby birds? Or because they are birds in the first place? Or do you think it is wrong for the snake to want to eat them? Remember that birds are a normal part of a rat snake's diet. If it doesn't eat these particular ones, then he certainly will eat others that he can find. Besides, I would like to see what the robins are going to do."

We went back to the porch and watched for a while. Bill got out my binoculars, and sat with them rested on the rail, watching at close range the attacks on the suffering snake. The rain continued throughout the entire day without letup. The robins continued throughout the entire day attacking the snake in defense of their nest. Sometimes the female would dive, while the male fed the babies in the nest. Then the male would begin to harass the reptile and the

138

female took over the duty of caring for the fledglings.

The snake clung to the branch and took his punishment. Several times during the day Bill or I would go down to take a look at the scene of battle. By late afternoon the entire back of the snake was a mass of bloody punctures. In several places actual pieces of flesh had been pecked away.

The entire drama was unnatural to me. It is certainly not normal for a snake not to attempt to flee immediately on sight of a human being. Whether or not it was natural for one to take the amount of punishment this one was enduring I cannot say, but I sincerely doubt it. Anything unnatural in the animal kingdom is well worth observing, and so we kept this incident under our close attention for its duration. Several times we went to the tree, and actually put our hands on the snake's back. It merely tightened up at the touch, taking a fresh grip on the branch with its lateral folds.

The only answer that I could come up with was that the snake was so famished that it was desperate. Either it had been unable to find food, or had been unable to capture any. If the latter, it might be because it was sick in one way or another, since rat snakes are most capable hunters. Whatever the cause, the entire day, dull, chill because of the never-ceasing downpour, was spent in enduring the ceaseless assault by one parent bird or the other. Then Bill pointed to the reptile's head. I bent over for a closer look and saw that the lower jaw was twisted a little sideways. Then it came to me. Either the snake had met with a foe too strong for it, or some person had come across it and struck it with a stick or other weapon. The lower jaw was either broken or so twisted that the animal could not capture or hold its prey.

Now the reason was clear why the creature was

enduring a situation it otherwise would not. It was simply a matter of survival. It had two choices, feed or perish.

When dusk finally arrived the birds resorted to habit and stayed at the nest. My sympathies were with the snake, but I was determined not to interfere with the now tense drama being enacted in my own yard. The female robin sat on the nest to keep her chicks warm and dry. The male took up a guard station on the branch nearby. Darkness slowly lowered, and finally we could no longer distinguish details at the tree. An occasional chirp came from one or the other of the robin pair, as they settled in for the night. Not a sign of motion or life from the snake below.

When full night had fallen, Bill and I took a flashlight down to the scene. The snake was still stretched along the branch. It had loosened its grip, but as we came up to it with the light, it again threw the lateral loops about the limb to afford better purchase.

We shone the light up and saw the two glistening black eyes of the mother bird, huddled close down into the nest. The male was still at his post on the branch.

First thing both Bill and I did in the morning was dash down to the tree. The rain had stopped during the night. All was silent. The snake was gone. A few dark stains on the branch told the mute story of its ordeal. The nest was empty and both adult robins were gone. Bill stooped and picked up two stiff tail feathers. They, too, told a story.

I wondered if two adult robins and a few tiny chicks would sustain the serpent until it was able once more to find food and capture it.

Appendix:

Animals and the Law

A large number of creatures have become extinct in the world since life began. Many of them have succumbed to natural evolutionary happenings. But only too many others are victims of the depredations of the human race.

Extinction is a thing of great finality. Once a species has been killed off entirely, it means that never— never in all time—will that animal ever be seen again.

Extinction leaves a hole in the ecosystem of whatever area it inhabited. Sometimes this hole closes up without much notice being taken by the remaining species. Sometimes it requires a sizable upheaval of natural processes to close the gap. In any event, the loss is irreparable, and, when man is to blame, it is a thing of shame and sorrow.

The federal Department of the Interior has compiled a list of all mammals, fish, birds, invertebrates, reptiles, and amphibians which are in danger, from one cause or another, of becoming extinct. It goes without saying that everything possible should be done to preserve these creatures and to give them another chance to rebuild their populations. If you want a copy of the list of endangered species, a letter addressed to the following department will bring one to you:

Office of Endangered Species and International Activities
Bureau of Sport Fisheries and Wildlife
U.S. Department of the Interior
Washington, D.C. 20240

Very few of the endangered animals are apt to appear on your property. However, in addition to animals which are recognized as endangered, there are many others that require protection to some degree to maintain stable populations, and these include some of the most common animals.

Thus many species of wild animals are protected by law. An animal which is so protected may not be kept captive unless the person keeping it has obtained permission and a license from his state's department of conservation. Some animals may not be kept at all, and no permit can be obtained for them.

If you want to keep an animal you have found around your home, get in touch with the department of conservation and ask for information concerning the animal. If an injured or juvenile specimen is found, a call to the department will put you in the clear as far as the law is concerned, and probably yield valuable information to help you in caring for the creature.

A list of state departments is appended here, together with a summary of each state's regulations.

ALABAMA
Director, Department of Conservation
64 North Union Street
Montgomery, Alabama 36104

All animals are protected except beaver, which is not mentioned in the lists available. Permits for keeping animals are not mentioned.

ARIZONA

Director, Game and Fish Department
P.O. Box 9095
Phoenix, Arizona 85023

A permit is required to keep any animal in Arizona.

ARKANSAS

Director, Game and Fish Commission
Game and Fish Building
Little Rock, Arkansas 72201

All animals are protected and require a permit except the bobcat and the wolf.

CALIFORNIA

Director, Department of Fish and Game
1416 Ninth Street
Sacramento, California 95814

A permit is required for all animals.

COLORADO

Director, Department of Game, Fish and Parks
6060 Broadway
Denver, Colorado 80216

Mink, otter, opossum, muskrat, beaver, weasel, squirrels, marten, porcupine, woodchuck, bats, moles, fisher, deer, and rats are not mentioned in protected lists.

Certainly deer and bear must be restricted as big-game animals. Animals named as under protection are: raccoon, skunk, fox, rabbit, bobcat, lynx, coyote, wolf, and chipmunk.

CONNECTICUT

Director, Board of Fisheries and Game
State Office Building
Hartford, Connecticut 06106

A permit is required to keep any animal.

DELAWARE
Director, Board of Game and Fish Commissioners
Box 457
Dover, Delaware 19901

Animals not mentioned in the protected list are: skunk, weasel, red squirrel, flying squirrel, marten, porcupine, bobcat, lynx, woodchuck, bats, moles, fisher, coyote, wolf, chipmunk, rats, and bear.

Animals which are protected are: mink, otter, raccoon, muskrat, beaver, fox, gray squirrel, fox squirrel, rabbit, and deer.

FLORIDA
Director, Game and Freshwater Fish Commission
620 South Meridan
Tallahassee, Florida, 32304

A permit is required for any animal.

GEORGIA
Director, Game and Fish Commission
401 State Capitol
Atlanta, Georgia 30334

Animals not mentioned in the protected list are: beaver, fox, marten, bobcat, lynx, porcupine, woodchuck, bats, moles, fisher, coyote, wolf, chipmunk, and rats.

Animals under protection are: mink, otter, raccoon, opossum, muskrat, skunk, weasel, all squirrels, rabbit, deer, and bear.

IDAHO
Director, Fish and Game Department
600 South Walnut, Box 25
Boise, Idaho 83707

Protected animals are: mink, otter, muskrat, beaver, marten, deer, and bear.

Unprotected animals are: raccoon, opossum, skunk, weasel, fox, squirrels, rabbit, porcupine, bobcat, lynx, woodchuck, bats, moles, fisher, coyote, wolf, chipmunk, and rats.

ILLINOIS
Director, Department of Conservation
102 State Office Building
Springfield, Illinois 62706

Protected animals are: skunk, muskrat, opossum, raccoon, otter, mink, weasel, fox, gray squirrel, fox squirrel, rabbit, woodchuck, and deer.

Animals not mentioned in the lists are: beaver, red squirrel, flying squirrel, marten, porcupine, bobcat, lynx, bats, moles, fisher, coyote, wolf, bear, chipmunk, and rats.

INDIANA
Director, Department of Natural Resources
603 State Office Building
Indianapolis, Indiana 46204

Permits are required for any animals.

IOWA
Director, Iowa Conservation Commission
East 7th and Court Avenue
Des Moines, Iowa 50319

Animals not protected are: red squirrel, flying squirrel. Animals not mentioned in the lists are: marten, porcupine, bobcat, lynx, bats, moles, fisher, wolf, bear, chipmunk, and rats.

Protected species are: mink, otter, raccoon, opossum, muskrat, skunk, beaver, weasel, fox, gray squirrel, fox squirrel, rabbit, woodchuck, deer, and coyote.

KANSAS
Director, Forestry, Fish and Game Commission
P.O. Box F
Pratt, Kansas 67214

Unprotected animals are: all squirrels, woodchuck, bats, moles, fisher, coyote, chipmunk, and rats.

Protected species are: fox, weasel, beaver, skunk, muskrat, opossum, raccoon, otter, mink, marten, lynx, bobcat, porcupine, rabbit, deer, wolf, and bear.

Permits are available to keep protected species as pets.

KENTUCKY
Commissioner, Department of Fish and Wildlife Resources
State Office Building Annex
Frankfort, Kentucky 40601

All animals are protected except the gray fox and the woodchuck. Licenses are required to hunt any animal. Permits are required to keep any animal.

LOUISIANA
Director, Wildlife and Fisheries Commission
400 Royal Street
New Orleans, Louisiana 70130

The only animal listed as unprotected is the fox. All other species are protected. No information as to permits was available.

MAINE
Commissioner, Department of Inland Fisheries and Game
State House
Augusta, Maine 04330

This state pays a bounty on bobcats, which are totally unprotected. Species which are protected, but for which permits are issued to keep them as pets, are: raccoon, skunk, and fox.

Protected species are: mink, otter, muskrat, beaver, gray squirrel, rabbit, fisher, deer, and bear. Scientific permits may be obtained to keep these animals.

Animals which are completely protected, and for which no permits are issued, are: marten and lynx.

MARYLAND
Director, Department of Game and Inland Fish
Box 231
Annapolis, Maryland 21404

Animals not listed are: flying squirrel, marten, fisher, coyote, wolf, and bear. Unprotected animals are: weasel, porcupine, bobcat, lynx, bats, moles, rats, and chipmunk.

Protected species are: beaver, skunk, muskrat, opossum, raccoon, otter, gray and red squirrels, fox, mink, rabbit, woodchuck, and deer.

MASSACHUSETTS
Director, Division of Fisheries and Game
100 Cambridge Street
Boston, Massachusetts 02202

All animals are protected in this state. Permits are not mentioned.

MICHIGAN
Director, Department of Conservation
Stevens T. Mason Building
Lansing, Michigan 48926

Bear, deer, and flying squirrels are not mentioned. Unprotected species are: skunk, opossum, weasel, red squirrel, bats, moles, porcupine, chipmunk, and rats. The state pays a bounty on coyotes.

Protected animals are: mink, otter, raccoon, muskrat, beaver, gray squirrel, fox squirrel, rabbit, bobcat, and woodchuck. Permits can be obtained for these species. Animals which are completely protected, and for which permits are not issued, are: marten, lynx, fisher, and wolf.

MINNESOTA
Commissioner, Department of Conservation
301 Centennial Building
St. Paul, Minnesota 55101

Unprotected species are: raccoon, opossum, skunk, weasel, red squirrel, porcupine, bobcat, lynx, wolf, and bear.

Species not mentioned in protected lists are: woodchuck, bats, moles, coyote, rats, and chipmunk.

The fisher and marten are under complete protection in this state. Other protected animals are: mink, otter, muskrat, beaver, gray squirrel, fox squirrel, rabbit, and deer.

This state issues permits only for scientific study, according to my information.

MISSISSIPPI
Executive Director, Game and Fish Commission
P.O. Box 451
Jackson, Mississippi 39205

Several species are not mentioned in the literature sent me by this state. They are: marten, porcupine, lynx, woodchuck, bats, moles, fisher, coyote, wolf, chipmunk, and rats.

Unprotected animals are: beaver, fox, and bobcat.

Protected species are: skunk, muskrat, opossum, raccoon, otter, mink, weasel, all squirrels, rabbit, deer, and bear. Permits are available for all these species except bear, which is completely protected.

147

MISSOURI
Director, Department of Conservation
P.O. Box 180
Jefferson City, Missouri 65102

Unprotected animals are: red and flying squirrels, marten, porcupine, fisher, moles, bats, lynx, woodchuck, rats, wolf, chipmunk, and coyote.

Protected species are: fox squirrel, gray squirrel, weasel, fox, beaver, skunk, muskrat, opossum, mink, otter, raccoon, rabbit, bobcat, deer, and bear.

MONTANA
Director, Fish and Game Department
Helena, Montana 59601

Animals not mentioned in protected lists are: raccoon, opossum, fox, all species of squirrels, rabbit, porcupine, and lynx.

Unprotected species are: skunk, weasel, bobcat, woodchuck, bats, moles, rats, coyote, wolf, and chipmunk.

Protected animals are: mink, otter, muskrat, beaver, marten, fisher, deer, and bear.

NEBRASKA
Director, Game, Forestation, and Park Commission
State Capitol Building
Lincoln, Nebraska 68509

The state of Nebraska protects all animals. Hunting licenses are issued during the seasons for certain game animals. All other animals may be kept only by permit.

NEVADA
Director, Fish and Game Commission
Box 678
Reno, Nevada 89510

This state does not issue any permits for any animal.

NEW HAMPSHIRE
Director, Fish and Game Department
34 Bridge Street
Concord, New Hampshire 03301

All animals are protected in this state except two. Permits are available to keep animals as pets. This state pays a bounty on bobcat and porcupine.

NEW JERSEY
Director, Division of Fish and Game
Department of Conservation and Economic Development
Box 1390
Trenton, New Jersey 08625

Unprotected species are: opossum, skunk, and weasel. All other animals are protected. Permits are available.

NEW MEXICO
Director, Department of Game and Fish
State Capitol Building
Santa Fe, New Mexico 87501

Under complete protection are: gray, red, and fox squirrels, woodchuck, deer, and bear. No permits are available. No other species are mentioned in protected lists, which apparently means any other than those mentioned above could be kept as pets.

NEW YORK
Director, Fish and Game, Conservation Department
State Office Buildings, Campus
Albany, New York 12226

Not mentioned in the lists are: flying squirrel, fisher, and wolf. Unprotected animals are: opossum, weasel, fox, red squirrel, porcupine, bobcat, lynx, woodchuck, bats, moles, coyote, rats, and chipmunk.
   Protected animals are: all other species. Scientific permits for study are available for all these except marten, which is under complete protection.

NORTH CAROLINA
Executive Director, Wildlife Resources Commission
P.O.Box 2919
Raleigh, North Carolina 27602

Skunk, weasel, and bobcat are unprotected. All other species are protected, and permits for pets are issued.

NORTH DAKOTA
Commissioner, Game and Fish Department
103½ South 3rd Street
Bismarck, North Dakota 58501

Permits are required to keep any animal as a pet.

OHIO
Department of Natural Resources
1106 Ohio Departments Building
Columbus, Ohio 43215

Otter and marten are not mentioned in the lists for this state.

Unprotected animals are: flying squirrel, porcupine, bobcat, lynx, bats, moles, fisher, coyote, wolf, chipmunk, and rats. The state pays a bounty on fox.

Protected species are: mink, raccoon, opossum, muskrat, skunk, weasel, gray, red and fox squirrels, rabbit, woodchuck, deer, bear, and beaver.

OKLAHOMA
Director, Department of Wildlife Conservation
P.O.Box 53465
Oklahoma City, Oklahoma 73105

Deer and bear are not mentioned in protected lists. All other animals are unprotected.

OREGON
Director, State Game Commission
Box 3503
Portland, Oregon 97208

Permits are required and available for all species of mammals except the following, which are under complete protection: fox, skunk, bats, deer, and coyote.

PENNSYLVANIA
Executive Director, Game Commission
P.O.Box 1567
Harrisburg, Pennsylvania 17120

Animals not mentioned in protected lists are: marten, lynx,

bats, moles, fisher, coyote, wolf, and rats.

Unprotected species are: weasel, fox, flying squirrel, porcupine, and chipmunk.

Protected animals are: beaver, skunk, muskrat, mink, otter, raccoon, opossum, gray, red, and fox squirrels, rabbit, bobcat, woodchuck, deer, and bear.

RHODE ISLAND
Chief, Division of Conservation
Department of Natural Resources
83 Park Street
Providence, Rhode Island 02903

Permits are required to keep any animal as a pet.

SOUTH CAROLINA
Director, Division of Game
Wildlife Resources Department
Box 167
Columbia, South Carolina 29202

All species of mammals are protected. Permits for pets are not mentioned in the lists.

SOUTH DAKOTA
Director, Department of Game, Fish, and Parks
State Office Building
Pierre, South Dakota 57501

Protected species are: mink, gray squirrel, fox, weasel, beaver, skunk, muskrat, raccoon, opossum, bobcat, deer, coyote, and bear. No other species are mentioned in the lists.

TENNESSEE
Director, Game and Fish Commission
Room 600, Doctor's Building
Nashville, Tennessee 37203

Animals not mentioned in protected lists are: mink, otter, skunk, beaver, weasel, fox, red, and flying squirrels, porcupine, lynx, bats, moles, fisher, rats, wolf, coyote, chipmunk, and marten.

Protected animals are: raccoon, opossum, muskrat, fox, gray squirrel, rabbit, bobcat, woodchuck, deer, and bear.

TEXAS
Executive Director, Parks and Wildlife Department
John H. Reagan Building
Austin, Texas 78701

Not mentioned in protected lists are: beaver, weasel, flying squirrel, marten, rabbit, porcupine, bobcat, lynx, woodchuck, moles, fisher, and chipmunk.

Bats, rats, coyote, and wolf are not protected. All other species are protected, and permits are not mentioned.

UTAH
Director, Division of Fish and Game, Department of Natural Resources
1596 West North Temple
Salt Lake City, Utah 84116

Otter, mink, marten, beaver, rabbit, deer, and bear are protected, but may be kept as pets with a permit. All other species of mammal may be kept without a permit.

VERMONT
Commissioner, Fish and Game Department
Montpelier, Vermont 05602

Unprotected animals are: fox and bobcat. Protected species are: flying squirrel, rabbit, marten, porcupine, lynx, bats, moles, fisher, deer, coyote, wolf, rats, bear, and chipmunk.

All other species of mammals are under complete protection.

VIRGINIA
Executive Director, Commission of Game and Inland Fisheries
Box 1642
Richmond, Virginia 23213

Virginia issues scientific permits only for the following animals: muskrat, opossum, raccoon, otter, mink, beaver, fox, all squirrels, and rabbit.

Species which are unprotected are: skunk, weasel, marten, porcupine, bobcat, lynx, woodchuck, bats, moles, fisher, deer, coyote, wolf, bear, rats, and chipmunk.

Deer and bear are probably restricted, even though they are not listed in the state literature.

WASHINGTON
Director, Department of Game
600 North Capitol Way
Olympia, Washington 98501

Not mentioned in protected lists are: opossum, fox squirrel, rabbit, woodchuck, bats, and moles.

Unprotected animals are: skunk, beaver, fox, porcupine, coyote, and rats.

Protected animals are: mink, otter, raccoon, muskrat, weasel, gray, red, and flying squirrels, marten, bobcat, lynx, fisher, deer, wolf, bear, and chipmunk.

WEST VIRGINIA
Chief, Fish and Game Division
Department of Natural Resources
State Office Building, 3
Charleston, West Virginia 25305

Unprotected animals are: opossum, skunk, weasel, fox, red and flying squirrels, bobcat, porcupine, lynx, woodchuck, bats, moles, rats, and chipmunks.

Animals which are not mentioned in the lists are: marten, coyote, and wolf.

Protected species are: mink, muskrat, beaver, raccoon, gray and fox squirrels, rabbit, fisher, deer, and bear. The otter is completely protected.

WISCONSIN
Conservation Administrator, Division of Conservation.
Department of Natural Resources
Box 450
Madison, Wisconsin 53701

Permits are required to keep any animal as a pet.

WYOMING
Commissioner, Game and Fish Commission
P.O.Box 1589
Cheyenne, Wyoming 82001

All mammals are protected and permits are available for pets.

There are also offices throughout the Canadian Provinces dealing with animals and wildlife. For those readers who live in Canada, I list these addresses:

CANADIAN GOVERNMENT
Chief, Canadian Wildlife Service
Ottawa, Canada

ALBERTA
Fish and Wildlife Division, Department of Lands and Forests
Edmonton, Alberta, Canada

BRITISH COLUMBIA
Chief, Game Management
Fish and Game Bureau
Parliaments Building
Victoria, British Columbia, Canada

MANITOBA
Director of Wildlife
Department of Mines and Natural Resources
Winnipeg, Manitoba, Canada

NEW BRUNSWICK
Chief, Fish and Wildlife Bureau
Department of Lands and Mines
Fredericton, New Brunswick, Canada

NEWFOUNDLAND
Director of Wildlife
Department of Mines, Agriculture and Resources
St. Johns, Newfoundland, Canada

NORTHWEST TERRITORIES
Deputy Commissioner of N.W.T.
Vimy Building
Ottawa, N.W.T., Canada

NOVA SCOTIA
Fish and Game Association
P.O.Box 654
Halifax, Nova Scotia, Canada

ONTARIO
Chief, Fish and Wildlife Bureau
Department of Lands and Forests
Parliaments Building
Toronto, Ontario, Canada

PRINCE EDWARD ISLAND
Director of Fish and Wildlife
Department of Industry and Natural Resources
Charlottetown,
Prince Edward Island
Canada

QUEBEC
Director of Wildlife Division
Department of Tourism, Game and Fish
Quebec, Canada

SASKATCHEWAN
Director of Wildlife
Department of Natural Resources
Government Administration Building
Regina, Saskatchewan, Canada

YUKON TERRITORY
Game Department, Yukon Territory
White Horse, Yukon Territory, Canada

The following addresses are the regional directors of the United States. Each director covers a number of states.

REGION ONE
Includes: Alaska, California, Hawaii, Idaho, Montana, Nevada, Oregon, and Washington.

Address
Regional Director, Bureau of Sport Fisheries and Wildlife
U.S. Department of the Interior
730 NE Pacific Street, P.O.Box 3737
Portland, Oregon 97209

Wild Animals Around Your Home.

REGION TWO
Includes: Arizona, Colorado, Kansas, New Mexico, Oklahoma,
   Texas, Utah, and Wyoming.

Address
Regional Director, Bureau of Sport Fisheries and Wildlife
U.S. Department of the Interior
Federal Building, P.O.Box 1306
517 Gold Avenue, Southwest
Albuquerque, New Mexico 87103

REGION THREE
Includes: Illinois, Indiana, Iowa, Michigan, Missouri, Nebraska,
   Ohio, North and South Dakota, and Wisconsin.

Address
Regional Director, Bureau of Sport Fisheries and Wildlife
U.S. Department of the Interior
Federal Building, Fort Snelling
Twin Cities, Minnesota 55111

REGION FOUR
Includes: Alabama, Arkansas, Florida, Georgia, Kentucky,
   Louisana, Maryland, Mississippi, North and South Carolina,
   Tennessee, Virginia, and District of Columbia.

Address
Regional Director, Bureau of Sport Fisheries and Wildlife
U.S. Department of the Interior
Peachtree-Seventh Building
Atlanta, Georgia 30323

REGION FIVE
Includes: Connecticut, Delaware, Maine, Massachusetts, New
   Hampshire, New Jersey, New York, Pennsylvania, Rhode
   Island, Vermont, and West Virginia.

Address
Regional Director, Bureau of Sport Fisheries and Wildlife
U.S. Department of the Interior
U.S. Post Office and Courthouse
Boston, Massachusetts 02109

Index

amphibians, 68–69
anoles, 96–97
armadillos, 63–64, 121–125

baby animals, 12
bats, 17
bear, black, 101–102
beavers, 43–44, 61
behavior patterns in animals, 36
birdfeeders, squirrels at, 45
bird spiders, 65
birds, 31, 37, 38–40, 42, 45–46,
  70–73, 106–110, 137–140
birds of prey, 130
bites, danger of, from wild
  animals, 17, 20, 128, 129
black widow spiders, 66
blind snake, 84
bluejays, 45
bobcats, 56

Bronx Zoo, 116
bulb flowers, destruction of, by
  chipmunks, 30
bull snakes, 85
butterflies, 40

captive animals as lures, 37,
  119–120
chameleons, 96, 98–99
chewing and gnawing damage by
  squirrels, 24–25
chickens taken by predators, 49,
  51, 53, 54, 70, 73
children, adoption of wild
  animals by, 11–14, 115–116,
  128–130
chipmunks, 24, 30, 53, 58
confinement, fear of, in animals,
  19–20
copperheads, 69, 76, 79–80

Index

coral snakes, 69, 76, 80
corn snakes, 85
coyote, 54
coypus, 60–61
crops, unharvested strips of, to attract wildlife, 43

daddy longlegs, 65
damselflies, 66
darning needles, 66
deer, 28, 42, 43, 44, 63, 100
deer mice, 27, 48
DeKay's snakes, 84
Department of the Interior, U.S., 141–142
destruction of crops and trees by mice and deer, 28
diseases transmitted by animals to humans, 17–18
dobsonflies, 66
dogs, 34, 62, 113
dragonflies, 66

eagles, 130
ecological balance, 16
endangered species of animals, 141–142 ff.
ermine, 52
extinction of animal species, 141

feeding wild animals, 14, 33–35, 104, 112, 114, 116, 117–118, 120, 123, 126, 129, 132, 135–136
fence swifts, 96
ferrets, 50
field mice, 27, 48
fleas, 18, 132
flying squirrels, 60, 130–133
foxes, 17, 53, 102–106

garbage as wild animal food, 14–15

gardens, animal damage to, 43, 48, 56–57, 61, 62
Gila monsters, 87–88
girdling of trees by mice and deer, 28
groundhogs, 56

habitat, invasion of, by man, 12–14, 15–16
harvestmen, 65
hawks, 70, 73, 130
hellgrammites, 66
hognosed snake, 68, 81–82, 95–96
horned toad, 88–90
hourglass spiders, 66
housebreaking wild animals, impossibility of, 114

injured animals, 36, 102–103
insects, 64–68
instincts in animals, 38–40
nesting, in birds, 107–111
See also behavior patterns
Isle Royale (Lake Superior), wolves of, 54

kestrels, 73, 130

lizards, 69, 87–90, 92–94
"lost" animals, 12
lures, use of, to attract animals, 37
lynx, 54–55

marmots, 56
marsupials, 133
meadow mouse, 27–28
mice, white-footed (deer mice), 26, 27, 48
house, 27
migratory birds, 37–38, 40
mites, 18

milk snakes, 85
minks, 52
misinformation about wild
    animals, 10–11, 14–15
moles, 28–29, 48
monogamy in animals, 105
mountain lions, 56

nectar-feeding birds, 39–40
nutrias, 60–61

opossums, 42, 73, 115, 133–136
orchards, damage to, by deer, 63
otters, 49–50
owls, 70, 71, 130

parasites, 18
"parrot fever," 17
partridges, 70
pheasants, 70
phoebes, 31, 106–110
picking up animals, 19–20, 126
plantings to attract wildlife, 42–
    43
poisons, use of, against animal
    pests, 32
ponds, use of, to attract wildlife,
    42, 43, 49, 61
porcupines, 62
'possum, see opossums
predators, 36, 39
psittacosis ("parrot fever"), 17

quail, 70

rabbits, wild, 18, 30–31, 50
    cottontail, 63
    jackrabbit, 63
rabies, 17
raccoons, 14–15, 16–17, 36, 42,
    48–49, 111–114
range of animals, 16, 49–69
    passim

rat snakes, 85, 137–140
Rat-I-Cator, 32
rats, 32, 40, 50, 51, 52, 69, 84
rattlesnakes, 69, 76–79
reptiles, see snakes
robins, 137–140

salamanders, 68
salt licks, 62, 63
scorpions, 64–65
shrews, 48
shrikes, 46
sickness in animals, indications
    of, 36
skinks, 69, 94
skunks, 11, 14, 17, 36, 42, 49,
    125–126
smoke, fear of, in animals, 20
snails, 70
snakes, 11, 18, 69, 74–87, 95–96,
    128–130, 137–140
sparrow hawks, 73
spiders, 65–66
squirrels, 17, 37, 45, 53, 70, 115–
    121
    red, 23–25, 60
    gray, 24, 59–60
    flying, 60, 130–133
streams, attracting wildlife with,
    61
structural damage to houses by
    squirrels, 25
suburban areas, animals in, 10,
    11
swifts, see fence swifts

talking to animals, 35–36
tarantulas, 65
teaching animals, 118
ticks, 18
toads, 68–69, 88
tularemia, 18, 63
turtles, 70, 90–92

Index

veterinarians, 18
voles (meadow mice), 27–28

waterfowl, 42
water moccasins, 69, 76, 80–81
watersnakes, northern, 128–130
weasels, 50–51
whipsnake, 86

wildcats, 56
winter, hardships of, for animals, 44
winter feeding, 37–38, 40–41, 44
wolves, 54
woodchucks, 42, 56–57
worm snakes, 84

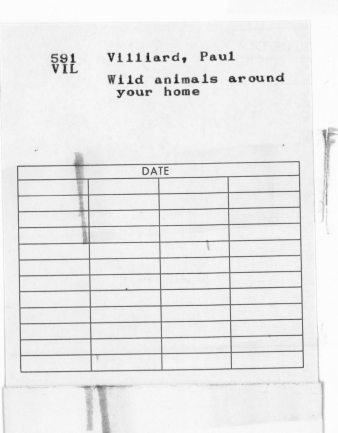

591
VIL

Villiard, Paul

Wild animals around
your home

DATE			